It's Not about the Gift

It's Not about the Gift

From Givenness to Loving

Anthony J. Steinbock

ROWMAN & LITTLEFIELD
INTERNATIONAL

London • New York

Published by Rowman & Littlefield International, Ltd.
Unit A, Whitacre Mews, 26-34 Stannary Street, London SE11 4AB
www.rowmaninternational.com

Rowman & Littlefield International, Ltd. is an affiliate of
Rowman & Littlefield
4501 Forbes Boulevard, Suite 200, Lanham, Maryland 20706, USA
With additional offices in Boulder, New York, Toronto (Canada), and London
(UK)
www.rowman.com

British Library Cataloguing in Publication Information
A catalogue record for this book is available from the British Library

ISBN: HB 978-1-78660-825-3
ISBN: PB 978-1-78660-826-0

Library of Congress Cataloging-in-Publication Data

Names: Steinbock, Anthony J., author.
Title: It's not about the gift : from givenness to loving / Anthony J. Steinbock.
Description: Lanham : Rowman & Littlefield Publishers, 2018. | Includes bibliographical
    references and index.
Identifiers: LCCN 2018014822 (print) | LCCN 2018018768 (ebook) | ISBN 9781786608277
    (Electronic) | ISBN 9781786608253 (cloth : alk. paper) | ISBN 9781786608260 (pbk. :
    alk. paper)
Subjects: LCSH: Generosity. | Gifts.
Classification: LCC BJ1533.G4 (ebook) | LCC BJ1533.G4 S74 2018 (print) | DDC 128/.4--
    dc23
LC record available at https://lccn.loc.gov/2018014822

∞™ The paper used in this publication meets the minimum requirements of
American National Standard for Information Sciences—Permanence of Paper for
Printed Library Materials, ANSI/NISO Z39.48-1992.

Printed in the United States of America

For my sister, Teresa

Contents

Introduction

It's Not about the Gift is a strange title for a work that seems to deal explicitly with the problem of the gift. Certainly, the matter of the gift, of giving, of gift-giving is nothing new. We are long familiar with it from simple everyday exchanges with others (birthdays, Chanukah, Christmas, Eid, etc.), to practices of giving alms to the poor, to unspoken spontaneous acts of generosity, to stylized exercises of bonding in diverse cultures, to religious characterizations of God in the Abrahamic tradition.[1] Conceptually speaking, as Jason Alvis points out, the Proto-Indo-European term *ghabh*—from which we get "gift" and the German language gets "*Gabe*" (and related expressions like giving, givenness, *geben*, *Gegebenheit*, etc.)—implies the intersubjective dimension of giving and taking. Likewise, the French term *donner* [to give] derives from the Hittite expressions *dô* and *dâ*, meaning give and take.[2]

In liberation theology, the gift and gift-giving are seen as challenges to capitalism because generosity contradicts the logic of capital.[3] Others in political and critical theory have called attention to the unin-

---

1. On the latter point, see Robyn Horner, *Rethinking God as Gift: Marion, Derrida, and the Limits of Phenomenology* (New York: Fordham University Press, 2001). Augustine, for example, in *De Trinitate*, writes that "the Holy Spirit is the gift of God."
2. See, for example, the thorough study, Jason W. Alvis, *Marion and Derrida on The Gift and Desire: Debating the Generosity of Things* (Dordrecht: Springer, 2016), esp. Chapter 1.
3. See Gustavo Gutierrez, *A Theology of Liberation: History, Politics, and Salvation* (New York: Orbis Books, 1973).

tended negative effects of generosity even if giving is well intended.[4] The existentialist Jean-Paul Sartre, at a different end of the spectrum, considered the gift as subjugating and giving as a means to appropriate by destruction—although, as Ruud Welten has pointed out, for the Sartre of the *Notebooks*, the gift implies the reciprocity of recognition and the liberation from the world.[5]

Philosophically, the matter of the gift has assumed new proportions by virtue of the works of Jacques Derrida and, in particular, his reading of Marcel Mauss's cultural anthropological study on the potlatch and the gift. Is the gift and gift-giving mired in the circulation of exchange, and for essential or structural reasons? Does the gift *as such*, which is completely unconditional, eclipse its own possibility in an essential economy? Ensuing discussions and debates between Derrida and Jean-Luc Marion on the given, the process of being-given, and the "saturated phenomenon" have further raised the stakes in these philosophical investigations bearing on the gift. They bring with them the broad swath of the phenomenological tradition, which they presuppose, and the pervasive phenomenological concept of givenness. In particular, they retrieve Heidegger's thoughts on the "Event," the "It gives" or *Ereignis*, and Husserl's phenomenological reduction to "givenness."

I do not wish simply to recapitulate these discussions, which are already established as the canon of contemporary literature on the gift. Nor do I intend to rehearse those trenchant commentaries that contributed for us their own decisive insights and advanced our understanding of the central issues surrounding the problematic of the gift. I do however want to take up some of these key figures in the discussion and propose the following: The discussions of the gift are really *not about the gift*, or should not be mistaken to be about the gift. The gift is not the point because the gift only becomes the gift in the context of interpersonal loving.

From a different angle, the gift becomes a gift in humility, which is how we receive ourselves in loving. Derrida is correct to this extent, namely, when the gift is the end of giving, it disappears as such; when it is the object of giving, it cannot appear. This does not mean for me,

---

4. Romand Coles, *Rethinking Generosity: Critical Theory and the Politics of Caritas* (Ithaca, NY: Cornell University Press, 1997).

5. See Ruud Welten, "Jean-Paul Sartre, Notebooks for an Ethics: The Ontology of the Gift," *Journal for Cultural and Religious Theory* 15, no. 1 (Fall 2015): 3–15. See Jean-Paul Sartre, *Cahiers pour une morale* (Paris: Gallimard, 1983), esp. 297–98, 399, 433. And see Jean-Paul Sartre, *L'Être et le néant: Essai d'ontologie phénoménologique* (Paris: Gallimard, 1943).

however, that the gift is the cipher of the impossible. Rather, the gift becomes what it is only when it is the surplus, excess, or remainder, as it were, of interpersonal loving and not the object of loving. Moreover, the gift fully becomes the gift in the *intertwining* of the religious, moral, and aesthetic dimensions of experience, as de-limited vertically, as opening to and inter-implicating these other dimensions in their distinctive ways.

It is only in what we could call a natural attitude perspective that the discussion of the gift is about the gift, and as if *it* were the entry point and the goal of the deliberations, as if the entire issue were self-evident, even in our so-called deconstructive or phenomenological analyses of the gift. What is unnoticed in all this discourse about the gift is that it is *not about the gift*. For the gift to have appeared at all, it could not have been about the gift. My peculiar position is to intervene in the talk of the gift through selective interpretations that approach the problems of the gift and givenness, with the proviso that it is not about the gift. More specifically, I intervene in the contemporary discussion of the gift through a set of critical readings in which I situate in each instance the gift in interpersonal and inter-Personal relations.

I ask the reader's indulgence while I trace this problem of the gift through different styles, voices, approaches, and traditions—going from a phenomenological analysis, to expositions and critiques of Heidegger, Henry, Marion, Derrida, and in an admittedly curious move, back to Maimonides. The latter move is curious because this early medieval rabbinic scholar has not been part of this contemporary discussion. Yet it is Maimonides who offers us distinctions and discernments that bring the contemporary conversation forward. The guiding thread running through these accounts is the insight that what is at stake in the gift is our relation with others. Our relations with others are revealed in many ways, interpersonally, in what I have called "moral emotions," but most profoundly through loving. By loving, I understand a dynamic movement toward the emergence and flourishing of what is possible within this movement of being-becoming, given through value. Loving as movement is an improvisational, free, creative, positive affirmation, as generative of and beyond the givens in a personal manner. Loving then "participates the other" such that what is "given" is already revealed as beloved.

I treat the phenomena of loving, hating, and the beloved in a subsequent work. Here, I want to move from the gift to loving (loving, from which the gift originally emerges) in the following way. By offering a careful phenomenological analysis of the experience of surprise, I tease apart the gift from how it is usually accepted as tied to the surprise. Chapter 1 works through the ways in which the emotion of surprise accepts reality, believing what I cannot believe, articulating its temporal presuppositions of expectation and suggesting that the gift becomes the gift, not by being surprising, but by it being received in the moral emotion of humility. Humility, which is not given in a direct first-person reflection, is the way that the gift becomes gift without its being the object of an intention. Humility is the way in which I receive myself in loving—without I, Myself becoming an object of the reception, or the gift becoming the object of interpersonal loving.

Chapter 2 takes up the problem of the gift, brought into relief in Chapter 1, by confronting Martin Heidegger's association of *Machenschaft*, or "machination," with the Jews, while examining this constellation within the context of *Ereignis*. Following out the movement of the "It gives" that takes place as withdrawal in sending/extending-opening, I briefly consider Heidegger's reflections on the prospect of overcoming machination and the Jewish problem, turning to the related matter of giving and the task of overcoming metaphysics. After the explication of giving and the gift in the context of overcoming metaphysics and machination, I offer some critical observations, reintroducing into this explication the context of personal individuation and interpersonal responsibility.

The issue of a giving that withdraws in favor of the gift and the ensuing matters of machination and metaphysics from Chapter 2 is taken up in Chapter 3 in the thought of Michel Henry. Now, developed in different "religious" terminology, the matter of withdrawal, giving, and the gift is discernable explicitly as the problem of forgetfulness. Because for Henry, transcendence is given to itself, but excluded from the structure of immanence, self-givenness takes place in the mode of "revelation" as immediate, direct, absolute self-givenness. Through the self-hiddenness of the self-generation of absolute Life, the more one takes up the gift of exercising one's ability to be, the more the ego forgets "Life"—the more we as human beings forget, for Henry, that we are sons in the Sonship of the Father. What he calls "doing," especially mercy, may be touted as the way of overcoming primordial forgetfulness, but it is uncertain to what extent even this "gift" is nothing more than the self-accomplishment of absolute Life. That is, it makes us question, again, the place and role of individuation, transcendence, the world, and especially interpersonal loving in the so-called mundane sphere of givenness.

Chapter 4 focuses on Jean-Luc Marion's ambiguous and under-developed notion of the "poor" phenomenon as an expression of the mundane phenomenon. This chapter elaborates upon and interprets the poor phenomenon in relation to the mode of givenness Marion also calls "revelation"—revelation, which for Marion concentrates the four types of saturated phenomena. If the effect of the saturated phenomenon on the subject transforms the otherwise passive object into the gift, the giver of sense into the receiver, or the "gifted," then in what sense is the "poor" an original feature of phenomenality and not derivative of saturation? Are poor phenomena essential or contingent features of our existence? I propose several ways in which the poverty of the "poor" phenomenon can be understood and, to view it in a more integrated way, suggest that the concept of the saturated phenomenon would have to give way to verticality and the process of de-limitation, founded in loving.

The final chapter moves from Marion's intimation of the poor phenomena to his and Derrida's explicit phenomenology and deconstruction of the gift. These recapitulations of the problem of the economy of the gift (Derrida) and the reduction to givenness (Marion) serve as springboards to an account of the gift in Maimonides, Rabbi Moshe ben Maimon, the prolific Jewish philosopher from the 12th–13th centuries. His treatise on gift-giving not only anticipates the description of the gift in its economic circulation (Derrida) and the prospect of bracketing or reducing aspects associated with the gift (Marion), but advances be-yond these the idea of the gift as appearing most radically through participating with the other toward liberation.

Although there are different gradations of the gift serendipitously covering Derrida's worries of economy and Marion's reductions of the gift to givenness, the meaning of the gift is fully realized as gift through the direct involvement with other persons toward their liberation from material and spiritual limitations. In Maimonides, the highest form of gift and giving connects the religious and moral dimensions of experience and moves the matter of the gift into the framework of vertical loving—pertaining to all dimensions of reality, and where persons are concerned, between finite (human) persons and infinite Person or the Holy. I conclude this work with critical reflections on the transition from a philosophy of the gift to a phenomenology of loving.

I would like to acknowledge and extend my appreciation to several careful readers of this manuscript, readers who have given their valuable time, offering generous comments and criticism. They have contributed considerably to my understanding of the matters dealt with in this work in many ways: Leslie Brown, Ed Casey, Kevin Hart, Sara Heinämaa, and Art Luther. My gratitude also extends to Andrew Barrette for his detailed attention, diligence, and patience in generating this index.

Chapter 1

Surprise, the Gift, and Humility

Although the experience of surprise is prevalent in everyday experiences and seems to be self-evident, it is a distinctive experience that is anything but clear. Indeed, although many philosophers and scientists of different traditions do mention it as a crucial experience, surprise as a theme has not been dealt with systematically in philosophy (or in the sciences). In contemporary literature in which the gift becomes a topic of discussion, the gift is commonly and simply assumed (somehow) to be coupled with surprise. In this chapter, I am interested in how surprise is related to a gift and the essential, crucial distinctions between them.

To do this, I want to ask: Does surprise have an affinity with perceptual and general epistemic functions and acts? What is its relation to the future? Does it have an epistemic import? Is surprise an affect? An emotion? What is surprise's relation to moral or interpersonal emotions? It would be too ambitious to respond in detail to all of these questions, but I do want to bring them into focus by determining surprise within the problem-field of feeling and then situate it in relation to the gift.

More specifically still, I examine surprise in terms of its belief structure, clarifying it as a believing what I cannot believe and, ultimately, distinguishing it from a startle (1). I then suggest that surprise is a being caught off guard, which is related to being attentively turned toward something (2). As the latter, I qualify surprise as an emotion in its being thrown back on an experience (3). This constitutes surprise as a disequilibrium in distinction to a diremptive experience like we find in the moral emotions of shame or guilt (4). Finally—and contrary to a common interpretation—I distinguish a surprise, which presupposes an expectation, from a gift, which is peculiar to the experience of humility and which (while it has its own futural temporality) is that in which precisely nothing is expected. I then suggest that surprise is an emotion although being neither an affect, like a startle reflex, nor a moral emotion, like shame, guilt, or humility.

1. THE BELIEF STRUCTURE OF SURPRISE

Surprise can be characterized by a peculiar relation to being. Allow me to describe this relation by examining its "belief structure," especially where the future is concerned. I do this because it is commonly held that surprise is simply a rupture of what is expected.

Expectation: Acceptance of What Is to Come

Within the phenomenological tradition, we discern temporal modes of time-consciousness relating to the present, the past, and the future. Where the future is concerned, we can observe a "protention," or an anonymous sketching out of the future that is based on a present occurrence and how that occurrence was retained as past. This takes place without any egoic activity or explicit attention to what is to come; it takes place through the "passive synthesis" of sense. An expectation is similar to a protention insofar as it is open to a futural occurrence arriving in the present, and it is also unfurled from the present and the past. Expectation is different from protention, however, insofar as expectation is an active comportment toward the future. In relation to this, we can see how an anticipation can be a more intensive attentiveness to the futural event.

For example, as I run to Times Square on New Year's Eve, my steps protend an even pavement; I place one foot in front of the other without even thinking of it. All of this happens as I expect the taxi to come to a stop so I can cross the street, and this takes place as I anticipate with bated breath the ball to drop in Times Square. These are all distinctive orientations toward the future, even though they all may be lived simultaneously. Now, to discern how surprise is dependent upon this futural orientation in the latter's various modes, let me describe the belief structure inherent in such a futural temporal mode of givenness.

For the sake of simplicity, let's stay with an expectation. Intrinsic to the act of expectation is the fact that the existence of something futural is posited. Expectation is carried out in the mode of belief as an unbroken, straightforward relation to something in the future. When I see the police car in my rearview mirror with its lights flashing (after I know that I have been going too fast), I expect the police car to pull up behind me and signal for me to pull over. When I expect this, I implicitly posit the existence of the officer, the police car, the lights, the forthcoming ticket, and so on. That is, the being of the officer, and so forth, is accepted in terms of the sense or meaning it has as going to come to pass; I live in the mode of natural, straightforward acceptance. This is another way of saying that when I expect something, I expect it as actually going to happen, not as something possible, or as possibly going to happen.

When I see the police car I "posit," or accept, it as actually behind me and as going to pull me over; when it speeds past me, going after the car in front of me, I accept with relief its actual passing, its "going to pull over that car." Further, expectation in all of its forms is not a rupture of belief; it is another kind of belief as a mode of time-consciousness, a straightforward one oriented in the direction of future actuality. In expectation, I count on the futural event as it is foreshadowed in the present. Thus, expectation is a temporal belief-act that is oriented toward the future as a mode of time-consciousness; it arises as motivated on the basis of, is demanded by, what has occurred in the present and is immediately retained as past.

Now, there are ways in which this straightforward futural acceptance can be modified or modalized. For example, something can be given as *possibly* going to occur, as *likely* to happen, as *probably* going to arrive, and so forth. For instance, I believe that the experiment to confirm the existence of the Higgs boson will probably work. Or, if there are too many counter-indicators—let's say that the equipment malfunctioned—I am *doubtful* it will work this time. The point here is that likelihood, possibility, probability, even doubt, are all kinds of belief postures or modes of belief. Aristotle seems to place the phenomenon of surprise here. In the *Poetics*, Aristotle connects *ekplektikon/ ekplexeos*—which can be translated as "surprise" or "being *struck* in "awe" or "astonishment"—with subjective discoveries through probable incidents.[1] *Thaumaston*, from *thaumazein* or wonder, on the other hand, is more open for the improbable; in fact, it is produced through improbable (or unexpected) incidents in relation to one another, which yields a great epistemic effect.[2] Wonder [*thaumaston*] for Aristotle, then, is a different phenomenon and cognitively "higher" than surprise [*ekplektikon/ekplexeos*]—both related to the probable and improbable.

Initially, we might want to say that surprise is the experience of the unexpected and, in this way, it may well sever its relation to belief. Adam Smith, for example, distinguishes between three "sentiments" that can initiate philosophical inquiry: wonder, surprise, and admiration. Wonder is excited by the new and novel; admiration is provoked by the beautiful; surprise is motivated by the unexpected, which for him is tied to the sudden, but not the rare.[3] Where Edmund Husserl's phenomenology is concerned, Smith's surprise would be a "disappointment," whereas Smith's wonder would be a "discordance."[4]

I Believe What I Can't Believe

Let's return to the experience of surprise in relation to an expectation. How do we characterize its peculiar belief-structure? When we are surprised, it often feels like an "I can't believe it," an "I can't believe what has just happened," or an "I can't believe what is happening." This experience entails a being caught off guard. This is why we can be surprised even in relation to ourselves (i.e., I can also surprise myself): "I can't believe what I just said" (say, I lost my temper, but I never lose my temper!) or "I can't believe what I just said; I know I said it" (I accept it), "but it goes against what I expect of myself."

The expressions given above that we find in our everyday experience are important clues to the experience of surprise, but if we were to

---

1. Aristotle, *Poetics*, ed. and trans. Stephen Halliwell (Cambridge, MA: Harvard University Press, 1995), 1454a 4; 1455a 17. Regarding wonder [*to thaumazein*] as the beginning of philosophy, see Aristotle, *Metaphysics*, Books I–IX, trans. Hugh Tredennick (Cambridge, MA: Harvard University Press, 1993), 982b 12–17.

2. Aristotle, *Poetics*, 1452a 4–6; 1460a 12–14. See 1460a 26–27: "Things probable though impossible should be preferred to the possible but implausible." Impossibilities are justifiable if they make that portion of the work more astounding (1460b 23–29).

3. Adam Smith, *The Early Writings of Adam Smith*, ed. J. Ralph Lindgren (New York: Augustus M. Kelly, 1967), esp. 30–31, 33, 39. Wonder is an elaboration of surprise, concerning the singularity of the succession.

4. See Edmund Husserl, *Analyses Concerning Passive and Active Synthesis: Lectures on Transcendental Logic*, trans. Anthony J. Steinbock (Dordrecht: Kluwer, 2001), esp. Part 2, Division 1.

remain simply with this aspect of the experience, it would conceal the deeper process of the constitution of sense in surprise. By "belief," I understand a basic "doxic" attitude, posture, or disposition that accepts the being of what arrives, has arrived, and what is to come in a straightforward manner. In this respect, "belief" does not have to be an active reflective commitment to or positing of being, but it can be a "presupposing" or "passive-positing" of being in a kind of pre-predicative "taking in" what takes place or what is.

With this understanding, we can more accurately portray what is happening in surprise. Surprise can be characterized as a movement of an "I am now believing what I could not believe at first," or again, "I am somehow accepting what I can't (in other circumstances) accept," or "I am living what I did not expect." In short, we have an "I believe what I can't believe," "I accept what I can't accept." For example, I never expected a birthday party, but here it is! Or more tragically, I can't believe she took her own life; she seemed so happy and successful, but she did commit suicide! In surprise, it is as if what happens comes out of nowhere, precisely because it is otherwise than the expected flow or unfolding of what is to come. But for the event to be experienced *as* surprise, *I must still accept it*. Thus, in surprise, there is an overall *reconstitution* or *reconfiguration* of sense where the event in question is concerned.

Accordingly, surprise, even on this descriptive level, is more complex and more "pre-reflective" in its doxic posture than, say, Donald Davidson or Daniel Dennett portrays it.[5] Davidson is too judicative, holding that surprise is the realization that the previous belief was false in the sense that there is an objective reality independent of previously held beliefs.[6] On the other hand, Dennett is partially correct when he writes that "Surprise is only possible when it upsets belief," but he does not specify how surprise is also the acceptance of this so-called "upset."[7]

If the "I can't believe" were entirely decisive and not encompassed with an "I now believe what I didn't believe would happen," then we would have something like a *shock* instead of surprise. Here, the event would not be reconstituted and reintegrated in its belief-attitude. In this

5. I would like to thank Natalie Depraz for bringing these works to my attention.

6. Donald Davidson, "Rational Animals," *Dialectica* 36 (1982): 318–27. And Donald Davidson, *Problems of Rationality* (Oxford: Oxford University Press, 2004).

7. Daniel Dennett, "Surprise, Surprise," commentary on O'Regan and Noe, *Behavioral and Brain Sciences* 24, no. 5 (2001): 982.

case, we would experience an "I cannot accept what I cannot accept." If there were not an acceptance of what I cannot otherwise accept—if the rupture of the straightforward relation to such a peculiar event were not accepted in some way—I would not live this experience as a surprise.[8]

Epistemically, we might want to classify surprise under the category of a disappointed perception, a disappointment that arises through a short-term or long-term rupture or discordance that is gradually reconstituted in sense. But in part because of its severity and intensity and in part because it issues in an immediate reconstitution of sense, surprise is distinctive from a disappointment. Put in more Husserlian colorful terms, we could say that surprise is the experience of the "shattering" of the noema, the sense-content of my ongoing intentional acts. Such a shattering of the noema in surprise is exemplified in the film *The Crying Game*: when Fergus (Stephen Rea) discovers that his new lover, Dil (Jaye Davidson), is a man, not a woman! What is demanded is a radical reconfiguration of sense, a new one supplanting the old (Husserl also writes of being "thrown from the saddle"). As is the case with any like reconfiguration of sense, the presence of the previous sense is retained, not erased, but as retroactively crossed out in its very reconfiguration as it is held on to in the past in the retention or primary passive condition of remembering.[9] For this reason, in surprise we find constituted an acceptance of what occurs against all expectation. This is one reason why surprise is something other than a mere disappointed or discordant perception, where certain aspects are modified only to yield a coherent sense of the whole.[10]

Thus, we can discern two moments of the surprise-experience in relation to its belief structure. On the one hand, there is a "being caught off guard," a radical "otherwise" in relation to expectation and the unfolding of sense: as otherwise expressed in the "I can't believe,"

---

8. I do not consider here the protraction of a shock or the relation of shock to trauma, how it can be repressed, and so on. Nor am I considering the experience of grief as a possible subsequent response to surprise or shock. Hegel never uses the term "Überraschung" in his *Phänomenologie*. However, for experiencing consciousness (not absolute Subject), every new structurally distinct encounter would throw this consciousness back on its experience such that it provides a motive for a step back or rather discovery and reconceptualization. Perhaps "surprise" is a suitable term for the encounter of what seems incidental and alien to its own making (positing), rupturing its expectation, and being thrown back on experience, and then testing, experimenting, and eventually reconceptualizing it.

9. See Husserl, *Analyses*, esp. Part 2, §7.

10. See Husserl, *Analyses*, esp. Part 2, Division 1. There is no feeling necessarily in the latter, no existential import.

which is the noetic expression co-relative to the "shattering" or "explosion" of the noema or sense-content. On the other hand, there is precisely a belief, an acceptance of the very nonacceptance. In terms of the belief-structure, this rupture is more than a disappointment; nevertheless, this rupture is not decisive because it is encompassed by a belief in what I otherwise could not believe at first.

Startle and Surprise

I would like to distinguish further between a startle and a surprise. In a still different example, we can imagine being in deep concentration while reading a book, then, suddenly someone who just came in let the screen door slam! I jump; I am startled. The startle is certainly a response to an unexpected givenness, a rupture, and it is sudden; but the startle in this instance takes place affectively *without any reconstitution of sense*. This has to do in part with the instantaneity of the startle. That is, if surprise is a believing what I cannot believe such that it entails a reconfiguration of sense, and shock is an I can't believe what I can't believe as a resistance to the reconstitution of sense for my meaningful world, then startle is neither of these. Accordingly, startle can be viewed in two registers, a static and a genetic one. A startle is characterized temporally with a suddenness, "now." We have two possibilities as to its constitution. On the one hand, it is neither reconstituted nor integrated in a flow of experiences—even if it presupposes a futural protention—which is why we can be startled in the first place! But, on the other, if the startle is viewed over time in the flow of experiences, it can be said to be "integrated" in the flow, but now as a "mere" disruption or rupture (or discordance) in the otherwise concordant or harmonious flow of meaning. But this does *not* mean that its presence demands a reconfiguration of the sense to be a startle.

Here, startle takes place under the threshold of the surprise and the shock. It is not a matter of not believing what I can't believe (shock) or believing what I can't believe (surprise). A startle takes place on a purely passive level of experience, and this is why it is appropriate to speak in terms of a startle *reflex*.

The question of suddenness has been a tricky issue in traditional descriptions of the surprise phenomenon. For example, in *The Passions of the Soul*, Descartes considers wonder [*admiration*] to be the first among the six passions. When we judge something to be new or very different from what we formerly knew or what we supposed that it ought to be, it surprises us, and this causes us to wonder.[11] Hence, Descartes can write that "wonder is a sudden surprise of the soul."[12] It is wonder that makes the soul consider the objects with attention—objects that seem to it rare or extraordinary. Notice that it is surprise that is even more "primary" than wonder and is itself founding for wonder. Further, Descartes's statement can be read in such a way that surprise is itself not essentially connected to the sudden. For Descartes, surprise arises from a judgment of something being new or quite different. So although surprise for him is connected to novelty and founded in a judgment, it is ambiguously tied to suddenness. When surprise is sudden, it issues in wonder.[13]

For me this is a clue. Although suddenness as a temporal experience can accompany surprise, suddenness need not accompany the rupture of experience to have an experience of surprise.[14] From a phenomenological perspective, it is startle that is essentially tied to suddenness, not surprise. Let's take another example, this time of the experience of a jack-in-the-box. I want to maintain that we are startled, not surprised, when we—especially when we were children—turn the crank of a jack-in-the-box: we know that "jack" is going to pop out, we turn and turn the crank, we wait and wait (we expect, without knowing precisely when), and then "pop!" out springs "jack." In fact, if "jack" does not pop out (something goes wrong), we will become disappointed (and maybe surprised, but not startled). This is similar to buying a ticket to go on a haunted house ride: we know we will be scared (or startled!), but we are not surprised by what happens. In fact, we expect it. Again, we might instead be surprised (and certainly disappointed) if the so-

---

11. René Descartes, *The Passions of the Soul*, trans. Stephen Voss (Indianapolis, IN: Hackett Publishing Company, 1989), Art. 53. It is the first of six primitive passions, along with love, hate, desire, joy, and sadness. See also, Sara Heinämaa, "Love and Admiration (Wonder): Fundaments of the Self-Other Relations," in *Emotional Experiences: Ethical and Social Significance*, ed. John J. Drummond and Sonja Rinofner-Kreidl (London: Rowman & Littlefield, 2018), 155–74.

12. See Descartes, *The Passions of the Soul*, Art. 70.

13. In order of foundation we would find judgment, surprise, wonder, and attention. Natalie Depraz concludes that wonder is *the emotional immediate after-effect* of surprise, whereas attention is its cognitive aftereffect. See Natalie Depraz, "Surprise, Valence, Emotion: The Multivectorial Integrative Cardio-Phenomenology of Surprise," in *Surprise: An Emotion*, ed. Natalie Depraz and Anthony J. Steinbock (Dordrecht: Springer Publishers, forthcoming).

14. It is also interesting to observe that a startle has an immediate bodily resonance, usually expressed in a kind of "jump," a violent twitch or sudden reflex movement. Although surprise is often expressed in raised eyebrows, a widening of eyes, or a stepping back, I can still experience surprise without any such facial or bodily gestures.

billed haunted house were just an ordinary open house tour listed by a real estate agent as a ploy to get us to see the house. Similarly, when the officer in the police car in back of me turns on her lights, I fully expect her to pull me over, turn on her lights, and so on, but when she turns on her siren, I am startled.

Temporally speaking, therefore, we can say that although startle demands the temporal feature of suddenness, surprise does not. It is the suddenness of the jack-in-the-box that contributes to the startle, not the unexpected per se. By contrast, I can still be surprised without suddenness (contra Smith and possibly along with Descartes) or without the rareness or extraordinariness of the event (contra Descartes, but along with Smith). For example, it surprises me, and *continues* to surprise me, that my friend acted in this way and that he continues to act the way he does, though there is nothing sudden about this. If fact, it may not be entirely unexpected. Discrepancy, contrast with, and interruption of the expected are not necessarily sudden. If my friend's actions no longer surprise me, it is because they have been integrated into the familiar.

In short, a surprise has to be understood as more than an experience of an unexpected givenness, though it entails that, and it must be more than a startle. Whereas a startle does not necessarily entail a reconstitution of sense, but can issue in an integration of sense, whereas it is sudden and is a reflex (and can still remain passive in this respect), a surprise entails a reconstitution of sense, need not be sudden (it can have duration), and is minimally the initiation into egoic activity of some kind. In view of its epistemic import, surprise has been connected to discovery, wonder, and philosophical inquiry. But I think that there is more here. It also has *existential* import insofar as it allows us to go on when confronted with the blow of the unexpected. Rather than being stymied with the shock of the "I can't believe what I can't believe," surprise is the accommodation of us to the situation by being the acceptance of what I cannot accept. But this is not merely an epistemic posture; it does it through the sphere of *feeling*, which has its own style of cognition and evidence.

2. BEING CAUGHT OFF GUARD AND ATTENTIVE TURNING TOWARD

In the previous section, I considered surprise as a believing what I cannot believe, having placed it in the context of an acceptance of what is to come, and I distinguished surprise from a shock and a startle. Let me now examine what takes place in being caught off guard and in accepting what I can't accept in the experience of surprise. Determining this will have important implications for whether surprise is a purely passive experience (passive in Husserl's sense) or whether it takes place in transition to or within an active, egoic sphere.

We can recognize that just because a passive protention is interrupted, this interruption does not constitute a surprise. I noted earlier that a protention is a passive, pre-egoic sketching out of the future that is based on a present occurrence and how that occurrence was retained as past. For example, as I take notes while reading a book, my bodily comportment is directed implicitly to what follows—from sitting on the chair, to the movement of my hands and eyes as I continue to read (all of which may be fulfilled or disappointed by the oncoming events). Now, I go to take a sip of tea, reaching for my cup while still reading my book. The protentional threads of my hand guide me to where I last placed the cup, but I do not find it there.

All this can go on implicitly while still concentrating on reading a passage. Though the protention is functioning through and through without any explicit judgment or inference of this process, there is not necessarily the emergence of surprise if I do not find my cup. For instance, I may get frustrated and turn my attention to the cup and look around; at this point surprise has not necessarily emerged, either rupturing, calling into question, supplanting, or supplementing the temporal, kinesthetic process of the protention. Simply because things do not go according to how we expect them to run their course does not necessarily mean that it is surprising (or startling, for that matter).

Furthermore, I can have a fully "passive experience" that is affectively significant without any explicit turning toward anything attentively. For example, I am writing or concentrating while reading a book, and there is a light buzzing sound. I am feeling more and more tense, but I do not become aware of this until after it hits a threshold. I finally notice that I am tense and bothered or that the noise was getting under my skin and that it was the annoying air conditioner. Looking back on the situation, I realize what was happening passively, and I note *now* that then I was "affectively" sensing the noise but it never registered as such. Or we can take a different example. Let's say that I am driving and I am used to the repetitive thumping of my tires on the highway. This is affectively working on me, as it were; it becomes a protention of an irregularity that as a whole becomes so regular that its rhythm lulls me into expecting the irregular as regular, and I notice it only when it is no longer present.[15] When I do turn toward it attentively, I do so merely out of curiosity, but I am neither startled nor surprised.

Let me now address this last point, namely, the possibility of an attentive turning toward in the transition from passive synthesis of sense to a more "active" or "egoic" constitution of it. There are many kinds of such attentive turning toward, but only one that pertains to surprise. Clearly, a startle *can* serve as a transition to an active turning toward. A loud bang, for example, can be so affectively prominent that I immediately turn toward the door and notice it as such. Here, we might have a movement from preconstituted sense to actively constituted meaning of the door, where the door slammed shut and the person walked through it.

But a rudimentary transitional experience can also found in recollection. For example, I am listening to my friend speak about a special plant, and then the mention of "fern" recalls to me, affectively, my time in the old-growth forest, and I am called back actively in remembering the ferns in the coastal forest. Accordingly, an affective turning toward something coming into relief affectively can instigate a new experience and can provoke the emergence of a new object.

What is distinctive about surprise in this regard is that it may not only serve as a transition from what is passively given to what is actively experienced; it not only instigates a new experience in the reconstitution of sense, but in being thrown off guard, *it throws me back on the experience.* I can examine it further, I can become curious, but I do not have to do the latter for it to be a surprise. It is sufficient that in being turned toward the event, *I not only turn toward it*, but I am thrown back on that relevant segment of experience. This is an active turning toward and back on an experience through which surprise instigates egoic activity—even though the turning toward and being thrown back onto experience is not a voluntary effort on the part of the ego. In fact, being in control of the experience in this way would mitigate the

---

15. See Husserl, *Analyses*, esp. §§37–39.

very experience of surprise; indeed, the process of crossing out and the reconfiguration of sense that does take place, takes place passively, without my actively doing anything.

A basic point I would like to suggest here is that if surprise occurs, it can never occur as such on merely a "passive" level or as a mere rupture in prereflective passive, associative concordance. It will occur either as a transition from a passive level to an active awakening or function within the active sphere, issuing in an attentive turning toward. This also points to the passive level of experience on which the startle occurs and the more active meaning-context in which surprise occurs. Thus, I distinguish between the being caught off guard peculiar to the surprise experience and the startle, which is fully pre-egoic as an experience.

3. SURPRISE AS AN EMOTION

Husserl has shown that everything coming into relief as a unity of sense does so as an affective relief and as exercising an affective allure on the perceiver.[16] It is not necessary to repeat these investigations here; it is sufficient to note that surprise shares with aesthetic and kinaesthetic experiences an *affective tonality*. But what kind of affective tonality does surprise have? Is it merely an affect? Does it exhibit a distinctive valence? Can it be considered to be an emotion and, if so, in what sense? Can it be qualified as what I have described elsewhere as a moral emotion?

In Kant's *Anthropology from a Pragmatic Point of View*, we have a very indirect invocation of surprise. That is, surprise is used first as a synonym for the disruption of expectation through contrast in order to clarify wit, but later it is pressed into service to define an affect. Because an affect is rash, as in the German term for surprise, *Überraschung*, it is distinct from a passion [*Leidenschaft*].[17] "Affect is surprise through sensation," whereby the presence of mind or self-

---

16. See Husserl, *Analyses*, Part 2, Div. 3.
17. Immanuel Kant, *Anthropologie in pragmatischer Hinsicht*, ed. Karl Vorländer (Hamburg: Felix Meiner, 1980), §55, §74. "Der affekt ist Überraschung durch Empfindung, wodurch die Fassung des Gemüts (*animus sui compos*) aufgehoben wird." In Kant's *Kritik der Urteilskraft*, when discussing humor (the joke and laughter), he writes that "Das Lachen ist ein Affekt aus der plötzlichen Verwandlung einer gespannten Erwartung in nichts." Thus, it is an affect that arises from a sudden transformation of a tension-filled expectation into nothing. Immanuel Kant, *Kritik der Urteilskraft*, ed. Karl Vorländer (Hamburg: Felix Meiner, 1974), §54.

control is suspended. Thus, surprise gives to a sensation "feeling" and "suddenness" to constitute the phenomenon of affect. Kant is therefore more ambiguous regarding the phenomenon of surprise, but nevertheless presupposes the "rush" of surprise to give *an affect* its suddenness (and open honesty) in contrast to the endurance (and hidden cunningness) of a passion.[18]

We can take this as a leading clue. Even if one wanted to challenge Kant's conclusions, or the more contemporary analyses and conclusions (by, say, Husserl, Merleau-Ponty, and others as well), which suggest that a perception is already affectively significant, we would be hard pressed to assert that surprise is affectively neutral. The fact that surprise is, well, "surprising!" already suggests that it bears some affective resonance in the very experience.[19] In a surprise, we are moved, and moved on the level of "feeling"! Before going further in terms of the status of surprise as an emotion or not, let me turn to its valence.

By valence, I understand the experience's positive, negative, or neutral tonality, or in general its "feeling-resonance." For example, when we experience shame, no matter what the shame is about, this emotion is always accompanied or colored by a negative valence. Even if we want to experience shame, it is this negative quality that we would desire. In a similar way, guilt is also qualified by a negative valence; it concerns a negative experience of a transgression of some kind. By contrast, hope is always given with a positive valence, as is loving. Whether pride is something we should or should not experience, it is always given with a positive valence. It would be possible to give other examples, but I want to turn to the instance of surprise.

The interesting thing about surprise where its valence is concerned is that its valence cannot be specified in advance. But this is not the same thing as saying that it is neutral. In a surprise, we are moved; a merely rational subject could never experience surprise. In surprise,

---

18. See Depraz, "Surprise, Valence, Emotion."

19. If we examine a discordance of an otherwise concordant experience, say, walking down the stairs while conversing with a friend, a misstep might constitute a *rupture* of that experience of walking, and if I am very much absorbed in the conversation, *I may not even notice* the misstep until after I reflect on what happened—how I scuffed my shoes, for example, or how I hurt my knee. Even if something is placed in my way and I trip, and then I regain my footing, this may be unexpected, it may be a rupture of my gait, but would this necessarily be constituted as a surprise? I don't think so; simply because things do not go according to how we expect them to run their course does not necessarily mean that it is surprising. That is, we could experience a rupture of experience, and this rupture or discordance (as an anomaly of concordance) could be integrated merely within a passive level of experience.

however, we can be moved in different ways. The experience of surprise can be given with a positive valence (a loved one shows up at my door), or a negative valence (my high school friend took his own life), or an indeterminate valence (my best friend just proposed to my sister, and "I don't know how I feel about that").

If startle is affectively significant, and only that, how do we characterize surprise? I suggest that surprise belongs to the sphere of emotions (and is not a mere affect). But if there is a more fundamental difference between surprise and startle, it is that surprise counts as an emotion: surprise is an *originating receiving* as an acceptance of what was not expected—a "receiving" in feeling—which does not mean that this is an active decision-making process. Surprise is more than an experience of an unexpected givenness and more than a turning toward an affective allure, and thus more than an affective life function. Rather, although surprise presupposes a rupture or a disappointed expectation and is at least a kind of turning toward as an initiation into "activity" and although a certain coming into relief affectively can be a prerequisite for surprise, the experience of surprise is still something different from that. It is a moved awakening to or turning toward, which is itself *an "original"* or *"creative" receiving within feeling*, a creative taking up of an affectively significant event, of emergent being or nonbeing in the unique manner of accepting what I can't accept, a being thrown back on the experience—as joyful, pleasant, hurtful, sad, and so on. It is creative in the sense that it is generative "improvisationally" beyond the givens. All this occurs without its being a process that takes place through a judgment or a reflection on the situation.[20]

Thus, surprise belongs to the sphere of the emotions insofar as it is more than the experience of a mere rupture, disappointment, nonfulfillment, or something unexpected, and as more than a startle reflex. It is an emotion in part because of the creative way in which we receive the situation in feeling through which we are moved. The fact that this or that could surprise or not suggests that it is operative on the level of the *person* in some sense. But this does not mean that surprise is lived as a

---

20. Hence, there is a fundamental difference between "I accept what I cannot accept" and an "I accept that I cannot accept." The former would characterize, in part, surprise; the latter only that my commitments do not entail what I thought they did, or alternately, a second order epistemic affirmation of what is not the case: "I believe that I can't believe that X is the case." The latter would not necessarily be the experience of surprise.

moral or interpersonal emotion.[21] In surprise, I am caught off guard and thrown back *on the experience*. I would now like to examine this aspect further by characterizing this folding back on experience as a "disequilibrium" in surprise and contrasting it with a "diremptive" experience, which occurs within some (but not all) moral emotions.

4. DISEQUILIBRIUM AND DIREMPTION

I distinguish surprise as an emotion from the field of moral emotions. By moral emotions, I mean those emotions that are essentially interpersonal or that arise in an interpersonal nexus (and not whether they are good or bad).[22] I have distinguished affects from emotions and specifically the moral emotions. Affects are feeling states and pertain to who we are as psychophysical beings, where we would find experiences like pleasure or pain, being ill at ease, tickling, and arousal. Here is where I place startle. Under "emotions," I include experiences like regret, remorse, fear, longing, and surprise (though this is only a sampling). These are emotions, without being moral emotions, because they can occur without any essential relation to personal "otherness" in that experience. They are genuine emotions, however, because they all presuppose an "order" or even "disorder" of the heart—to use a phrase from Pascal—and are lived in some way toward some other as bearer of value in a "creative" or personal manner.

To provide surprise with still sharper contours, I also want to distinguish its internal structure as an emotion from a set of moral emotions. Specifically, I characterize surprise as an *experience of disequilibrium* in distinction to the experience of moral emotions like embarrassment, shame, guilt, and the like, which are always *diremptive experiences*. The difference concerns, in the one case, being thrown back on the experience and, in the other, being thrown back on myself before another.

Diremptive Experiences

Let me begin with a diremptive experience. A diremptive experience is an experience in which I am given to myself as in tension with a basic

---

21. See Anthony J. Steinbock, *Moral Emotions: Reclaiming the Evidence of the Heart* (Evanston, IL: Northwestern University Press, 2014).

22. See Steinbock, *Moral Emotions*.

sense of myself as before another or others. In short, I am thrown back on myself before others in a way that calls me into question. Diremptive experiences are moral emotions, but not all moral emotions are diremptive experiences. For example, repentance, humility, loving, and trusting are not diremptive experiences, though they are moral emotions.

A diremptive experience can occur either as a mere infraction or rupture (an anomaly) in who I take myself to be or as a more substantial challenge to who I am. In the former case, we would have an embarrassment, namely, a "mere" discordance of a concordant dynamic orientation of who I am. Let's say that I show up at someone's house and discover that I have holes in my socks. If such a situation yields embarrassment (it need not, of course), it is because it is given as an infraction of my general character (for me) as someone who, for instance, takes pride in his socks. However, if it is only an infraction, it is because it is experienced as only an incidental breach. Importantly, however, it is sufficient to throw me back on myself as before another: I am usually well dressed, but now I have holes in my socks and my friends see it and I see them noticing it. I may apologize or make an excuse or simply turn red: I feel uncomfortable because this has violated in some way a sense of myself as before another.

Guilt, shame, and humiliation are other, more serious kinds of diremptive experiences. Let me focus on shame because of its kinship to embarrassment. Although shame is related to embarrassment as a diremptive experience, it is phenomenologically distinct. In this case, the diremption is lived as more than a mere infraction because the event or action threatens a "reconfiguration" of my character. On the one hand, there are now two (or at least two) competing ways of being, for example, on the one hand, a well-dressed person and, on the other, someone who cannot take care of himself or who may be "poor" (where poverty is accepted as a communal disvalue). The point here is that rather than the diremption being incidental in relation to who I sense myself to be, I experience it as a reflection on my character. However, even though there are two potentially competing orders or ways of being as a disorientation of my orientation, there is still "only" a threat of complete reorientation. This is because the two ways of being lived at this moment are not given on the same level; one is experienced as more basic than another. Instead, through shame, I am revealed to myself, before others or another, opening up the possibility of self-critique. Although shame is always an experience with a negative valence, shame may provide the possibility of a positive reorientation to who I "truly" am and thus open the possibility of a genuine self-critique. In short, without both of these, (1) this co-givenness or orientation and (2) without one being more basic, there would be no shame but merely alternative ways of being; I would not experience any kind of diremption at all.[23]

Now, let's examine the experience of surprise. I go over to a friend's house, take off my shoes, and find that I have a hole in my sock! What happened? I am surprised to find that I have such a hole because these were brand-new socks! *If* this is a matter of surprise, I can be surprised without its being before any other, real or imaginary. Further, surprise can take place without my being thrown back on myself at all. Certainly, I could subsequently reflect on what I did, namely, that I put on the wrong socks, that perhaps my shoe rubbed a hole in the sock, and so forth, but this is not essential to the experience of surprise. I could wonder about the being of sockness; I could admire my friend's beautiful new socks; I could pay attention to which socks I put on, and so on.

I characterize the surprise experience as a "disequilibrium" because I am "caught off guard" and thrown back *on the experience*, not on myself; I am before the experience, as it were, thrown back on the experience, but not necessarily before others and not necessarily *thrown back on myself*.[24] Instead, I am disoriented sheerly in relation to my previous orientation. In this way, surprise is neither a diremptive experience nor a moral emotion. In short, surprise does not reveal me to myself as before another, but it does catch me off guard and throw me back on the experience.

Surprise and Gift

It is commonplace to associate the gift and surprise. Even Jacques Derrida, known for his very careful and subtle analyses, will assert as if

---

23.   See Steinbock, *Moral Emotions*, Chapter 2. Shame and guilt (as well as pride) belong to the order of the emotions of self-givenness. Shame is self-revelatory (as is guilt), whereas surprise is not.

24.   Certainly, I can be thrown back on myself before "another"—where precisely I am that "other," like when I surprise myself (as in the example given above). This means that surprise can be a diremptive experience in certain circumstances. However, it need not be, and this is one reason that, although an emotion, it cannot be understood on the same order of embarrassment, shame, or guilt. I would like to thank Ellie Anderson for bringing to my attention this issue of a possible diremption within the experience of surprise.

it were self-evident that the gift, "if there is any," must harbor the structure of surprise precisely as irruptive and unforeseeable.[25]

An experience of surprise requires a futural orientation so that the latter be called into question. Although a necessary component, however, this is not all that is required for a surprise to emerge. If a surprise arises as something unexpected, it is in part because of the temporal mode of givenness that we can call generally an expectation. To delimit the experience of surprise further, I would like to distinguish the latter from the experience of a gift. I do this because we often associate a gift with something surprising. My point here is that, whereas *a* surprise (the thing, matter, or event) takes place correlative to the subject's experiencing surprise as an emotion, a gift arises correlative to the experience of humility as a moral emotion.

Although loving is an openness to any other (i.e., to all dimensions of being or reality, and in this sense, already "metaphysical"), it is most profoundly a personal movement and thus is given as a moral emotion; humility is the way in which we spontaneously receive ourselves (most profoundly) in loving. Like loving, humility is relational and reveals me to Myself as not self-grounding.[26] This revelation of Myself in humility ("Myself" as being given by another before another, as relational, as not self-grounding) is expansive and interpersonal such that I accept myself from another, as accepting the givenness from another and the contributions from others to what I do and to who I am. Thus, even if from the perspective of pride, I "lose" or "forget" myself, in humility, "I" receive myself as a recovery of Myself as relational because humility is the way I am self-given in the process of accepting or receiving. Unlike pride, humility is the experience of the not self-grounding character of who I am. Further, unlike other emotions of self-givenness, namely, pride, shame, and guilt, however, I am not self-given in a thematic way in humility. And unlike shame and guilt, I am not given to myself in a diremptive fashion. Instead, I am given as having received Myself.

I began with considerations of temporality, especially the mode of expectation, to explicate the experience of surprise. For something to be experienced as surprise, we have seen that an expectation must be in

---

25.   Jacques Derrida, *Donner le temps. 1. La fausse monnaie* (Paris: Galilée, 1991), 152–57; 186–90; 198. English translation by Peggy Kamuf, Jacques Derrida, *Given Time: 1. Counterfeit Money* (Chicago: University of Chicago Press, 1992), 119–23; 147–50; 156.

26.   For this notion of the "Myself," see Steinbock, *Moral Emotions*.

play. How is it the case for humility? What kind of temporal modes or modes of temporal givenness are in play? What is given in humility? It is important to recognize that not every futural opening of an experience is an expectation or founded in one. Hoping, for instance, has a different temporal meaning from an expectation. I do not expect or wait for something when I hope; rather, hoping is characterized as a sustainable and patient awaiting enduringly. Further, although I might be disappointed that a hoped-for object or event does not arise, I would not be surprised if the so-called impossible did not occur.[27]

The temporal mode of the future as an *expectation* is not in play at all in humility. That is, humility does have temporal meaning, but it has different temporal modes of givenness, which I have called elsewhere a presence-at, a remembering-ahead, and a devotion. That is, because humility (or being humble) is qualified as an openness toward and a reception of what is given, its mode of temporality relative to this openness and reception is a presence-at. This kind of presence-at is reflected in a being thankful for. Second, humility is not only related to the way in which something is accepted or received, but it is also a way in which I receive myself in and through being other oriented and the way in which I receive Myself as having been given to myself prior to being able to choose myself. If we understand receiving Myself in this way, then we can speak of a mode of givenness qualified as an "ante-memorial reception." Finally, because presence-at does not motivate anything new to come, it does not anticipate more to be thankful for and is not lived as an expectation. Nevertheless, there is a futural sense to humility, but this is related to a reception of what is given and of whatever is to come, without its being an anticipation of what is to come. Futurally, it is a kind of "accepting-ahead" without anticipated end. Accepting-ahead is not a mere passive experience but is lived "actively" as a devotion toward someone or something. Thus, even though humility is not oriented temporally, like an expectation, it does have a temporal meaning, namely, accepting-ahead as devotion.[28]

My main point here is that, in humility, I do not experience an expectation as one might find where it is an issue of a fulfillment of an intention, an anticipation of a return, or in general what we can call "just desserts." In being humble, I experience that I deserve nothing. To experience that I merit nothing is, however, *not* based on a depreciation

---

27. We could undertake a similar analysis for, for example, trusting or repentance. See Steinbock, *Moral Emotions*, esp. Chapter 5, regarding the experience of hope.
28. See Steinbock, *Moral Emotions*, Chapter 7.

of myself (in which case the focus would still be on myself), but rather in my devotion to some other, as it were, as received. In humility, I have no "just desserts" in the twofold sense that humility is not a matter of justice (as a third-party adjudication) and I do not dispose myself to another expecting something in return, with the attitude that I deserve this or that. Thus, there is no disappointment of expectation in humility. In fact, such a reception with no "just desserts" is what qualifies humility. There is no expectation of a fulfillment through what I intend, no disappointment, no rupture. Indeed, I cannot even regard myself as nondeserving then to have the experience be one of humility. Experiencing that I am nondeserving, for example, is possible only in and through the reception of the gift in humility; I cannot begin it as believing that "I am not deserving" before anything happens. That would be pride or self-denigration (which is another experience of pride).

In humility, there is no expectation of merit, and there is no expectation of return. Rather, there is nothing to expect. It is not *because of* humility that the gift emerges, but the gift emerges "in" humility. I cannot "intend" to be humble and have the experience of humility.[29] This is why disappointment is not operative in humility as a moral emotion. What is it that we experience in this situation? I suggest that it is not *a* surprise, it is not a rupture of an expectation, it is not the "unexpected," but what is received is received *as* gift. To expect nothing in humility means in the moral sphere that I deserve nothing in particular, which is why everything in humility is received *as gift*.

Likewise, when one receives in humility, what is received is received as a gift. Only post facto is it "humbling." Only after the fact do I feel myself as distinctly "undeserving." Again, humility admits of no intention, no fulfillment, no disappointment in the customary perceptual sense. Accordingly, Max Scheler writes that in humility one accepts all things with thanks, from the most subtle pleasure to the grandest bliss; we do this without ever imagining that we deserve even the smallest part.[30] The humble person does not give thought to the proper order of things, but accepts what comes with gratitude and without the thought of merit. Surprise, according to its peculiar structure, in accepting what I cannot accept, makes an initial gesture of rending something at our disposal. According to its essence, however, the gift is not at my disposal. It is true that the gift is received, but in the moment of its

---

29. See Steinbock, *Moral Emotions*, comparing pride and humility.
30. Max Scheler, *Vom Umsturz der Werte: Abhandlungen und Aufsätze*, ed. Maria Scheler (Bern: Francke Verlag, 1955), 18.

reception, it is not *as* at my disposal. It is the attempt to make the gift as something at my disposal that contributes to its disappearance as gift. It may well be that a gift requires a sacrifice. But if this is the case, then sacrifice (or offering) takes place on the part of myself as receiver, not on the giver. It is not the one who offers who loses something in giving, but the receiver who must have done so such that what is given is received as gift. What has been offered up, as it were, is the prideful self, but this has already been done through the acceptance of the other person. I "receive" Myself, but I do not "find" Myself.

Let's say that out of the blue we receive a love poem from an enemy. On one level, this same matter could be experienced as a surprise and yield an experience of surprise (where it might be a rupture of an expectation, be taken as unexpected, etc.), and on another level, it could be received as gift in the experience of humility, in which there is no expectation functional at all. As a whole, the poem could be experienced as a surprise gift. But these levels are phenomenologically distinct and in addition need not be given together. I can experience something as a surprise without its being given as a gift, and I can experience something as a gift, without its being a surprise. Thus, surprise as an emotion is not a moral emotion—as evident in its juxtaposition to humility—and a surprise is not reducible to a gift, and vice versa.[31]

The problem that gives rise to the identification of surprise and gift originates in part from ignoring the relation between loving and humility as distinctive moral emotions peculiar to persons in which the gift can appear as gift. My "intention" (contra Derrida) is not turned toward the gift—in which the gift becomes the figure of the impossible— because for us it is not a matter of intending a gift (see Chapter 5). In fact, *it is not about the gift.* Further, humility is not an "intention"—at least in any ordinary epistemic (i.e., perceptual or judicative) sense. There are indeed different modes of givenness.[32] To be sure, simply changing terms (from "intention" to "devotion") is not the point. The point, however, is the interpersonal relation in which the gift arises by

---

31. It could happen that I epistemically "expect" that someone may thank me for something I did for him (knowing his character), but in fact, I never expect anything at all for what I did, not even any kind of acknowledgment, and in this sense, "expecting thanks" does not even cross my mind.

32. See Anthony J. Steinbock, *Phenomenology and Mysticism: The Verticality of Religious Experience* (Bloomington, IN: Indiana University Press, 2007), "Introduction." And see Steinbock, *Moral Emotions*, "Introduction."

not aiming at the gift.[33] It is beyond surprise and nonsurprise. The "subject" does indeed not give or receive a gift because it is not about the subject and it is not about aiming at a gift; rather, it concerns the interpersonal nexus in which a gift appears as such and can only appear as such.[34]

CONCLUSION

My attempt in this chapter has been to delimit the experience of surprise and to examine some of its structural features in relation to the epistemic and emotional spheres. I have done this by examining surprise's relation to being as a belief-structure, namely, as an accepting or believing what I cannot believe. I then noted how surprise is a being caught off guard and an attentive turning toward, but in such a way that I am thrown back on the experience. Surprise as an emotion is distinct from a startle, which is operative as an affect in several respects: startle requires no reconstitution of sense, whereas surprise does, especially as *I am thrown back* on the experience in the latter; startle is always sudden, whereas surprise need not be marked by suddenness; startle can remain within the passive, anonymous sphere, whereas surprise is always operative either within activity or as a transition from the passive to the active levels of awareness; and startle is a reflex, whereas surprise as an experience is an emotion, presupposing an original or "creative" taking up or receiving of a situation.

Yet although surprise can be considered as an emotion, it is not a moral emotion. The former is marked by an emotional disequilibrium (constituted by being thrown back on an experience), which is distinct from being thrown back on myself before another, or what I call a diremptive experience (such as we find in certain moral emotions, such as embarrassment and shame). Finally, even though we might have something like a "surprise gift," a gift as such is given in and by the moral emotion of humility (which has a different futural temporality

---

33. It is true that receiving the gift can also be a transformation of the one who receives, but this already takes place in the presence of another. In pride, there is an exclusion of the gift through a rigidity of the self rather than a "being with" the other person. Receiving the gift, then, is an openness to the other as the openness to myself/ Myself, which means the transformation of Myself as open to the other person. It is essentially interpersonal. Ultimately, I receive Myself as from another, as not self-grounding.

34. Compare, Derrida, *Donner le temps*, 39; Derrida, *Given Time*, 24. See Chapter 5.

than an epistemic expectation) and is distinct from *a* surprise, which is given in the emotional experience of surprise and which still presupposes the temporal mode of expectation. I conclude that although surprise is neither an affective startle reflex, on the one hand, nor an interpersonal moral emotion, on the other, it still can count as an emotion. Finally, a surprise is essentially distinctive from a gift, which is received in humility.

Having teased apart the experience of surprise from the experience of the gift, I want to turn to the profound ways in which the gift and giving is taken up in the phenomenological tradition, beginning with Martin Heidegger. It is Heidegger who traces the problem of the gift and giving back to the eruptive event, *Ereignis*, but in the broader context of his thought, does so with some disastrous consequences.

Chapter 2

What Gives?

Heidegger, Machination, and the Jews

In this chapter, I examine Martin Heidegger's explication of giving and the gift in the context of his diagnosis of calculative thinking and overcoming metaphysics. I do this first by briefly underscoring his assertions on *Machenschaft*, or "machination" in relation to the "Jewish problem" (1). After treating the matter of gift and giving in terms of *Ereignis* (the spontaneous "event" taking place) (2), I conclude by making some critical observations on individuation, giving, the gift, and interpersonal responsibility within the context of Heidegger's reflections. Because I refer in part to Heidegger's *Schwarze Hefte*, or *Black Notebooks*, in this chapter, I want to make the following clarification of how I draw on Heidegger and these relatively recently published works.[1]

---

1. Thus far, the *Schwarze Hefte*, or *Black Notebooks*, make up three volumes of *"Überlegungen"* ["Reflections" or "Considerations"] and one volume of *Anmerkungen* ["Comments" or "Notes"]. They are edited by Peter Trawny. Martin Heidegger, *Überlegungen II–VI (Schwarze Hefte 1931–1938)*, Gesamtausgabe 94 (Frankfurt am Main: Vittorio Klostermann, 2014); *Überlegungen VI–XI (Schwarze Hefte 1938/39)*, Gesamtausgabe 95 (Frankfurt am Main: Vittorio Klostermann, 2014); *Überlegungen XII–XV (Schwarze Hefte 1939–1941)*, Gesamtausgabe 96 (Frankfurt am Main: Vittorio Klostermann, 2014); Martin Heidegger, *Anmerkungen I–V (Schwarze Hefte 1942–1948)* Gesamtausgabe 97 (Frankfurt am Main: Vittorio Klostermann, 2015). Hereafter, the Gesamtausgabe is cited as GA, followed by the volume and page numbers; all simple references to the GA will be cited in text.

I recall my first sustained exposure to the so-called "Heidegger Affair." I was a DAAD Stipendiat in Bochum, listening to the radio when a report came through about Heidegger's Nazi affiliation. The reporter was inspired by the new release of the Farías book.[2] The commentator had not only lambasted Heidegger, but also Michel Foucault and Jacques Derrida. How could Foucault, a radical leftist, challenging power relations, truth, and knowledge in radical ways—how could he read Heidegger? How could Derrida, the advocate of difference/*différance* have taken so much inspiration from this "Nazi"? What does this mean for *their and our* thinking? What does this mean for their and our *thinking*?

The overall point was that the Heidegger waters were toxic and, if one draws philosophical sustenance from these waters in any way, then the reader too will be poisoned. It is best then to avoid any contact lest we also become contaminated, even against our better selves. It also seemed to be imperative now to have no truck with any thinkers who had also drunk from those waters, be this thinker a Foucault, a Derrida, a Lévinas, or a de Beauvoir.

When the Farías book was first released, I recall thinking: "Should we reduce the meaning of a work to the life of the person? If the skeletons in one's closet are exposed, does it render his or her work suspect? Is *Sein und Zeit* inherently 'Nazi'? Is it anti-Jewish? And even if this were true, are we really so insecure in ourselves that we think reading a work will contaminate us or our own thought? Could Jews become anti-Jewish by studying Heidegger? Even if Heidegger were a Nazi, does it mean that his writings are fascist, National Socialistic, or even anti-Semitic?"

Not everyone was as naïve as this reporter. To the credit of certain philosophers in Germany at the time—at least where I was situated—those like Bernhard Waldenfels, Otto Pöggeler, and Elmar Holenstein and, in Wuppertal, Klaus Held—they did not go the route of such reductionism. Pöggeler unveiled his lectures on the then unpublished *Beiträge*,[3] and Held taught a seminar on *Langeweile* and tried to re-think Heidegger's philosophy of *Grundstimmungen* or fundamental

---

2. Victor Farías, *Heidegger et le nazisme*, trans. Myriam Benarroch and Jean-Baptiste Grasset (Paris: Verdier, 1987). Victor Farías, *Heidegger and Nazism*, trans. Paul Burrell and Gabriel R. Ricci (Philadelphia: Temple University Press, 1989).

3. See Martin Heidegger, *Beiträge zur Philosophie (Vom Ereignis)*, Gesamtausgabe 65, ed. Friedrich-Wilhelm von Herrmann (Frankfurt: Vittorio Klostermann, 1989).

moods in this context.[4] A bit later in Paris, I witnessed an effluence of books and discussions on Heidegger (François Lyotard, Jacques Derrida, Fransçoise Dastur—just to name a few), and in 1989–1990, École Normale hosted a special open seminar on the *Beiträge*, inviting a variety of speakers.

If the 1960s saw a first wave of reaction to this "Heidegger Affair" and the late 1980s witnessed a second wave, indeed, a virtual tidal wave of responses, then Heidegger's *Black Notebooks* are stirring waters that had regained their calm, agitating a third wave of reactions. In an article published in *Die Zeit*, after the appearance of the first three volumes of the *Black Notebooks*, the headline read: "Heideggers Schwarze Hefte: Das vergiftete Erbe" ("Heidegger's Black Notebooks: The Contaminated Legacy").[5] This new "wave" carries slightly different currents because on Peter Trawny's view, whereas the former two tides disclosed Heidegger's association with Hitler and National Socialism, the *Black Notebooks* reveal an anti-Semitism.[6]

Nevertheless, like before, the questions rear their heads again: Can one study Heidegger and not be contaminated by his works? Do Heidegger's convictions repudiate his work as philosophy? Can one study Heidegger without confronting his (political) past? Or again: Do these past and current revelations like we see in the *Black Notebooks* have anything to do with his philosophy?

We all might wonder how such a gifted thinker like Heidegger could have supported the Hitler regime, how he could have nourished the hope that National Socialism might establish his philosophical convictions in the political sphere, or even more specifically, how he could have believed that a conflict existed in any form between "the best blood of the best" of Germany's own people and "world Jewry."[7] We wonder this in part because we admire Heidegger, in part because we

---

4. Klaus Held, "Fundamental Moods and Heidegger's Critique of Contemporary Culture," trans. Anthony J. Steinbock, in *Reading Heidegger: Commemorations*, ed. John Sallis (Bloomington: Indiana University Press, 1993), 286–303. Peter Trawny, editor of the *Schwarze Hefte*, was also a student in Wuppertal at this time.

5. Thomas Assheuer, *Die Zeit*, N° 12/2014 (March 21, 2014).

6. See Peter Trawny, *Heidegger et l'antisémitisme: Sur les Cahiers noirs*, trans. Julia Christ and Jean-Claude Monod (Paris: Seuil, 2014). Peter Trawny, *Heidegger und der Mythos der jüdischen Weltverschwörung*, 3d ed. (Frankfurt am Main: Klostermann, 2015).

7. Heidegger, GA 96: 262. Although I appreciate the fact that some commentators prefer to translate "das Weltjudentum" as "world Judaism," I don't think Heidegger has the religious or ethical/practical sense of Judaism in mind in this context. For this reason, I prefer to translate this expression as "world Jewry."

take him as exemplary, and in part because we think that, of all people or at least of all thinkers, he should know better, he should *think* better. Without going the way of apologetics by asserting that the "thinking" we need to think is not even upon us yet to make sense of these avowals, we can still maintain that it is not only too easy, but both ingenuous and misleading for us to point the finger at Heidegger while supposing that we are somehow absolved from or not complicit in the general problem of evil.

My effort then is not to condemn Heidegger along these lines or to engage in a kind of apology, now in the context of the *Schwarze Hefte*, but to examine these issues critically within the context of giving and the gift.

1. MACHINATION

Machination [*Machenschaft*] (and what Heidegger will *mutatis mutandis* later term "*Gestell*" or "enframing") is expressive of the omnipresent rational, technical-scientific, and quantitative managerial control of all reality and the reduction of Beyng-historical [*seynshistorische*] Truth to efficacious problem solving. For Heidegger, it is not just a question of control or power, but the power of planning, of manipulation, of the holding sway of an insidious style of technological measure, perpetuated through a will to calculate and to quantify, a leveling out of everything qualitative and distinctive, which in its complexity becomes expressive of nihilism and metaphysics. Machination not only includes Dasein (Heidegger's modal term for the human being), robbing the "Beyng-historical Truth" of Beyng from the human being, rendering the latter world poor, and ordering Dasein into the category of beings as a whole; it is also perpetrated by the human being. As a consequence, we become the unwitting "tools" of the defeat of our own humanity. Human beings are not the makers of machination, but carry out machination as entangled in it, as the "last" expression of metaphysics. In the appearance of machination, human culture has reached its extreme, but it also thereby signals the possibility of a new beginning.

However brief his flirtation with National Socialism, Heidegger's attraction to it was related to what he perceived as a problem in the contemporary human condition. Although his own National Socialism was not aligned with Hitler's regime, this was not because he was critical of Hitler and National Socialism per se, but because the latter had not remained true to itself; instead, it had itself become swept up in the expansive technological power dominating the modern age that he called "machination," a power that he thought National Socialism would somehow be able to transcend in the political realm.

How does Heidegger's assessment of machination play into the problem of racism, anti-Semitism, the Jewish question, and the problem of the gift? It is indeed disconcerting that when Heidegger references certain thinkers of Jewish heritage, he mentions them precisely in the context of *racial* (and not spiritual) Judaism. For example, he mentions his former teacher, Edmund Husserl (Jewish by birth, but who converted to Protestantism), in the context of the putative increase of the power of Jewry, empty rationality, the aptitude to calculate, and the lack of ability to penetrate the realm of essential decisive resoluteness (GA 96: 46); he cites the "Jew 'Freud'" in the context of psychoanalysis reducing everything to life and instinct and whose thought is pure nihilism (GA 96: 218); and when discussing a Soviet diplomat as an example of the "underhandedness" of Bolshevik politics, he names the "Jew Litvinov."[8]

On the other hand, it is difficult to accuse Heidegger of racism, or in particular, of anti-Semitism because, according to Heidegger, the language of racism is itself expressive of machination and its drive to render everything calculable and manipulable; this kind of organization reduces everything to the organic as interchangeable; it reduces the expansive sense of culture and rootedness to a biologism that actually leads human beings, especially the German people, astray from their Beyng-historical mission (GA 96: 31, 213). In fact, in his *Black Notebooks*, the disparaging references to the "Bolsheviks" and "Christianity" are far more numerous than to the "Jews." But, as Heidegger himself observes in a different context, we should not succumb to machination's temptation of the quantitative and think that just because the references are less in number that they are therefore less significant.

The point here is that Heidegger stereotypically associates the Jews with the propensity for calculating and profiteering and therefore as-

---

8.   Heidegger, GA 96: 242. Maxim Maximovich Litvinov (1876–1951) was a Soviet diplomat, the "People's Commissar of Foreign Affairs" (1930–1939), and Soviet Ambassador to the United States (1941–1943). As a Jew, Litvinov was unable to represent the USSR to Hitler, so he was sent to the United States as an ambassador, thus for Heidegger putatively contributing to the worldwide proliferation of Judaic machination. I would like to thank Peter Trawny for this latter observation.

cribes machination, the alienation of Beyng to the Jews, Jewry, and to Judaism. Furthermore, unlike the Germans, who are rooted in soil and history, the Jews are homeless (evoking the typecast of "the wandering Jew"); unlike the Germans (or at least German philosophers), Judaism suffers from a so-called uprootedness, being putatively bound to nothing and therefore having a propensity to make everything serviceable or at its disposal (GA 95: 96–7, 282).[9] In short, the Jews (and presumably like everyone else and everything else) are caught up in and susceptible to the intoxicating matrix of machination, but they are also cast as the privileged conveyers of machination who facilitate the domination of modern technology on human beings and nature, draining themselves and everyone else of their Beyng-historical "existence" and of their "humanity."

Put differently, Jews were not for Heidegger a political or a racial problem, but a "metaphysical" problem because the Jews (among others of their ilk) are the symptomatic conveyers of the withdrawal, forgetfulness, or the abandonment of Being. Heidegger reflects: "The question concerning the role of *world Jewry* is not a racial one, but rather the metaphysical one." It concerns the type of humanity that can straightforwardly and nonbindingly "undertake as a world historical 'task' the uprootedness of all beings from Being" (GA 96: 243). Machination is not the Jews' fault, but because of their apparent similarity in structure, the Jews are presumably particularly adept at the machination's domination and can especially "prosper" in it. This seems to be the basis of Heidegger's disconcerting assertion in the "Anmerkungen" ["Comments" or "Notes"] of the fourth volume of the *Black Notebooks*—disconcerting no matter how one reads it—that the Jews are responsible for their own annihilation.[10]

So, for Heidegger, it is not simply a matter of world domination as the quantitative spread of Jews or Bolsheviks, et al., all over the earth, because machination is itself the "power" of quantitative manipulation

---

9. See also Martin Heidegger: *Die Grundbegriffe der Metaphysik. Welt-Endlichkeit-Einsamkeit*, Gesamtausgabe 29/30, ed. Friedrich-Wilhelm von Herrmann (Frankfurt am Main: Vittorio Klostermann, 1983), 261 ff. But such a characterization of worldlessness also strikes at his conviction that animals are "world poor" and thus reducing Jews to what he considers the world poverty of animals.

10. Heidegger, GA 97: 20: "Only when what is essentially 'Jewish' in the metaphysical sense struggles against what is Jewish is there attained in history the apex of self-annihilation; assuming that what is 'Jewish' has taken over the dominion everywhere completely for itself, such that even the struggle of 'what is Jewish'—and this above all—is brought under its sway."

and measured extension in which human beings become entangled and of which they are "thoughtlessly" the executors (GA 96: 6, 25, 30–2, 46–7, 48, 52–3, 111). The true danger is not world Jewry, but the exclusive "success" of machination in the metaphysical sense (metaphysical Judaism), the abandonment of the Being of beings through the forgetfulness of the Being of beings. This is why it cannot just be "world Jewry" that is implicated here as a metaphysical problem; like the latter, England, Americanism, pragmatism, liberalism, Bolshevism, and Christianity are oriented toward and play themselves out in the global unleashing of machination such that they (and we) live uncritically in the abandonment of Being (GA 96: 110–11).[11]

Machination was expressed in the war as technological prowess, power, and the will to calculate; it had further implications for reducing the earth to a resource under quantitative measure, bringing all beings under our dominion as controllable and at our disposition, as well as reducing human beings to the status of beings deprived of decisive resoluteness. In his sweeping critique of such machination in 1949, Heidegger's original version of the *Question Concerning Technology* maintained that the motorized food industry is essentially the same as the manufacture of corpses in the gas chambers and the death camps.[12]

Now, we all like to make connections and to detect structures that animate apparently disparate experiences. Who has not at the very least been struck by if not impressed with Horkheimer and Adorno's discernment of "Enlightenment Rationality" operative already in Homer's *Odyssey*, and with having read the domination of nature in Odysseus's act of having plugged the ears of his shipmates and bound himself to the mast while gaining knowledge from the Sirens? But do we not at the same time, at least with Heidegger, witness the loss of individuation and uniqueness of persons (despite his protests to the contrary) when equating the murder of even one person with the motorized food industry? A possible "animal ethics" not withstanding (where motorized

---

11. In a critical assessment of "sociology," Heidegger asks why "Jews and the Catholics" prefer doing sociology (i.e., rather than genuine Beyng-historical thinking). See Heidegger, GA 95: 161. That which is "Catholic," he writes as an obvious criticism, is absolutely "un-Nordic" and "completely un-German." See Heidegger, GA 95: 326.

12. This is from the original 1949 manuscript of Heidegger's essay "The Question Concerning Technology," as cited in Wolfgang Schirmacher, *Technik und Gelassenheit: Zeitkritik nach Heidegger* (Munich: Alber, 1983), 25: "Agriculture is now a mechanized food industry, in essence the same as the production of corpses in the gas chambers and exterminations camps, the same as the blockading and starving of countries, the same as the production of hydrogen bombs" (GA 79: 27/27).

food has evolved into fast food), are there no *moral* discriminations to be made? To Heidegger's credit, he had the good sense of excerpting this statement from the 1953 version of this work.[13]

Machination is expressed in the radical quantitative indifference and interchangeability of all beings, finding its political expression in popular movements like democracy, pluralism, liberalism, bolshevism, Christianity, mass communication, and so on (GA 96: 213). Although it is also expressive not only of the withdrawal of Being, but of our perilous forgetfulness of the withdrawal, for Heidegger, the extreme position of machination meant that we were (and presumably still are) also on the verge of something else, a new beginning, precisely in the possible recovery of the self-denying withdrawal. The recovery of the latter as openness to the mystery of Beyng, as the overcoming of machination qua metaphysics, should be the harbinger of a new sense of uniqueness that has no essential connection to the leveling out of all differences in terms of interchangeability and quantitative and technological control.

The task for Heidegger is to overcome the metaphysics of presence as the uncritical prevailing privilege of this way of Being. The question is not therefore whether Heidegger was anti-Semitic or a Nazi or whether we might become contaminated by his writings. The question for us, rather, bears on the structure of his thought given the problem of overcoming metaphysics, which amounts to overcoming machination. Related to this in different terms, can he guide us successfully to the matter of individual uniqueness (as he points to at times) and to individual and collective responsibility in the face of such uniqueness? Is "giving" appropriate to this task?

2. *EREIGNIS*, IT GIVES, GIFTS, AND WITHDRAWAL

I have attempted to grapple with some aspects of Heidegger's notion of individuation in the context of describing religious experience and moral emotions.[14] My conclusions (restricting them here to *Being and Time*) were that the individualzing at stake concerns Da-sein as a *mode* of being in relation to the ontological anonymity of *das Man* [the One].

---

13. Though we might wonder why he would want these other statements published in the *Schwarze Hefte* at all, let alone as his intended culmination of the Gesamtausgabe.

14. Steinbock, *Phenomenology and Mysticism*, esp. Chapter 6; Steinbock, *Moral Emotions*, esp. Chapter 3.

Thus, it concerns retrieving Dasein from its self-disorientation among other modes of being (e.g., being-ready-to-hand, being-present-at-hand), appropriating it *uniquely* as the there-being (Da-sein) of world disclosure—it does not bear on the concrete individual. Accordingly, although Heidegger speaks of guilt in both ontic and ontological senses, it cannot bear on the deepest sense of individuation that is both personal and interpersonal.[15] For the purposes of this work, I approach the question of individuation and the related issue of responsibility from another angle, namely, the matter of giving and the gift.

Although our unique access to Being in *Being and Time* was through that privileged mode of being called Dasein, the *Black Notebooks* suggest that to attain Being [*Seyn*] as freed from machination, that is, in its deepest sense as *Ereignis*, as eventing Event, we have to free ourselves of the being-ness of beings, which is to say, from the hegemony of beings.[16]

Years later in *Zeit und Sein*, Heidegger embarks upon this new approach more systematically in attempting to think Being without beings or even without this privileged mode of being, Dasein. He does this to evade the sway of machination and not to be misled from the start by reducing Being to a thing that beings have. It is an attempt to think Being outside of the framework, or better, outside the enframing of metaphysics. The problem according to the *Schwarze Hefte* is that beings (and all things intelligible in the field of beings) are beset by machination such that Being is in principle unintelligible for *thinking*; "ordinary" beings and culture renders the mystery of Being unapproachable. Recognizing the mystery of Being outside of calculative manipulation is the beginning of a new thinking, the openness to the *Unheimlichkeit* of Beyng (GA 95: 290–91; see also, GA 94: 196). The task, then, is to break with the realm of beings to be open to the event of Beyng, to follow the withdrawal of Being from beings by tracing Being to its "own" from *Ereignis*. To approach Being without beings and without regard to metaphysics is to be attentive to the *matter* of Being and to the *matter* of Time.[17]

15. See Steinbock, *Moral Emotions*, Chapter 3.
16. Heidegger, GA 96: 108: "Um vom Seyn als dem *Ereignis* er-eignet zu werden, müssen wir der Seiendheit des Seienden und der Vormacht des Seienden ledig sein."
17. Martin Heidegger, *Zur Sache des Denkens (1962–1964)*, Gesamtausgabe 14, ed. Friedrich-Wilhelm v. Herrmann (Frankfurt am Main: Kostermann, 2007), 29. English translation by Joan Stambaugh, *Time and Being* (New York: Harper and Row, 1977), 24. See also Françoise Dastur's analysis of this text, "Time, Event, and Presence in the Late Heidegger," *Continental Philosophy Review* 47, no. 3–4 (2014): 399–421.

In Shakespeare's "Hamlet," Polonius asks the brooding Hamlet, "What is the matter, my Lord?" (implying both "What is wrong?" and "What is the subject matter of your reading?"). And in a rather snarky, sarcastic reply, Hamlet quips, "Between who?"[18] Here, Shakespeare is playing on another sense of the term, "matter," namely, as a conflict or a tension in between. It is precisely this sense of the matter, or in German, *Sache*, to which Heidegger harkens when he characterizes Being and Time as "matters."

Being and Time are matters of thinking; they are not things, not beings. What is at stake is the relation "between" them (a "*Sachverhalt*") or that which issues them forth as matters: The relation relates Being and Time and yields [*er-gibt*] Being and Time (GA 14: 9/5). In this way, Heidegger approaches Being and Time not through temporal beings, but through the *giving*, the letting forth of Being and Time.

Although one could use the predicative form, Being "is" (here) or Time "is" (now), this would point to some particular thing that "is" in being or in time, reducing Being and Time to some*thing* before us. This would be misleading with respect to the givenness of Being and Time as matters for thought, as the "matter" that gives thinking and calls for thinking. Thus, Heidegger resorts to the expression "*es gibt*" Being, "*es gibt*" Time: literally, it gives Being, it gives Time (though the colloquial expression in American English is "there is" Being, Time, and so on, which again would not only presuppose Being, Time, and so on, but would render them accessible as objects potentially at our disposal). For this not to be a mere difference in idioms or a theme of ordinary language analysis, it is necessary for Heidegger to turn to the phenomenological *experiential* dimension of this expression and to describe the "It" and its "giving." How this *Es gibt* can be experienced and seen concerns the "how" of givenness of Being and of Time, that is, our relation to Being and Time without an appeal to beings (including Dasein).

Heidegger notes that from the very beginning of Western thinking, Being and Time are thought, but not the "*Es gibt*" that gives the gifts of Being and Time. How is it that we have missed the *Es gibt*? It is because, according to Heidegger, the *Es gibt*, the *It gives*, withdraws in favor of the gifts that It gives. This retreat opens the space for the gifts to be thought misleadingly and exclusively as Being with regard to

---

18. Shakespeare, *Hamlet*, in *The Complete Works of William Shakespeare*, ed. David Bevington (Glenview, IL: Scott, Foresman and Company, 1980), Act 2, Scene, 2, 194–95.

beings, conceptualizing Being as the ground of beings, as Time with regard to the present (as the punctual now or as the living present); Being and Time can then become the objects of thought, the possible projects of calculative manipulation at our disposal, in short, the province of machination (GA 14: 12/8). Although (and this can be seen as one of Heidegger's points) the fact that we could become forgetful of the giving at all such that Being as sending becomes being as present— the forgetfulness of Being—is testimony to the withdrawal/denial of giving in favor of the gift. Accordingly, there must be some sense in which machination is also "given."[19] I touch on this point again in my concluding section to this chapter.

Allow me to continue by noting that this giving that holds back in favor of the discernibility of the gift is qualified in a distinctive way. What is the nuance of this giving for Heidegger? This giving, which does not give itself, but only its gift, this giving that holds itself back and withdraws is called *sending* [*Schicken*]. In other words, the *way* of Being as letting-presence, and which in its own way belongs to giving, is a giving as sending and as a making place for. Thus, Heidegger can contend that the sending in the destiny of Being is characterized as a giving in which the sending source keeps itself back and thus withdraws from unconcealment (GA 14: 28/22). Being with regard to the grounding of beings is what is sent, Being is unconcealed (or more dynamically, unconcealing) in the concealing withdrawing of the It gives. It is when Being is disconnected from giving that the "metaphysics of presence" or Western thought only grasps the "gift" of Being as something present or as the "ground" of beings.

Similarly, Time is not present. Here Time itself—as in the case in machination—would avail itself to being managed ("time management") or saved like something I could possess ("saving time"), or designated as some period in time ("modern times"), or some slice of a day ("tea time"); likewise, Time is not mundane and measurable "clock time" ("what time is it?"). Rather, It gives Time as the temporalizing movement itself that cannot be contained as a moment "in time." Accordingly, the way of Time as letting-presence, and which in its own way belongs to giving, is a giving as extending that opens and conceals space-time (GA 14: 20/16). This is also why, for Heidegger, giving that gives time is determined by denying and withholding nearness: "An extending is itself a giving, the giving of a giving is concealed in

---

19. See Chapter 3 on Michel Henry concerning the problem of "forgetfulness."

genuine Time" (GA 14: 20/16; translation modified). Belonging to giving as sending, we can also find a keeping or holding back, which is a denial or removal from the living present.

This holding back/withdrawing/concealing therefore also designates a peculiar temporal structure of Being as sent. The holding back, the holding in abeyance, is epochal—as in the Greek, *epochē*. The *epochē/* epoch is the holding back—of "It"self for Being and Time. Each of its transformations (epochs) remains destined in this way such that the history of Being means the destiny of Being. Being is unconcealed for thinking with its epochal modifications, with its manifold sendings that in some way take place as history (GA 14: 12–14/8–10).

If Being and Time are unconcealed "gifts," then we can ask (to remain close to Heidegger's formulation): What withdraws in the granting as opening of Being-Time and preserves what remains denied in what has been? What is withheld in the approaching? In the expression "It gives," it is the "It" as giving. Heidegger capitalizes the impersonal "It" in the expression "It gives," not to determine the "It" as another kind of being or Being itself—in which case we would have the idea that Being gives Being—but to highlight a peculiar presence of an absence in the It gives Being and It gives Time.

Further, he attempts to gain access to the "It" (which is not a being or a present) by thinking the kind of giving that belongs to it—as noted above: the giving as sending, epochal destiny, as an opening up that reaches out [*lichtendes Reichen*] (GA 14: 21/18–9). To evoke the dynamic character of the It through its kinds of giving, Heidegger qualifies "It" further as *Ereignis*.

Ereignis is often translated in English as the Event of Appropriation to capture the sense both of "eventing," "occurring," "happening," and "belonging," "appropriating," "owning." I supplement this with a different translation that captures the sense of *Ereignis* in these two senses, namely, "taking place." However, although *Ereignis* is "Taking Place," it is not only an eventing through which there is a taking or appropriating. Deepening his earlier sense of truth as *a-letheia* or unconcealing-concealing, and retrieving the kinds of giving detected in Being and Time as noted above (sending/extending), Heidegger homes in on the It gives as *withdrawal*.

Accordingly, as much as *Ereignis* is an appropriating, *Ereignis* withdraws what is most fully its own from boundless unconcealing. Accordingly, "keeping back, denial, withholding—shows something like a self-withdrawing," what Heidegger terms, in short *Entzug* or withdrawal (GA 14: 27/22). Being and Time as matters relate (to) each other such that sending and extending are the *modes of giving* as determined by withdrawal. In the language of appropriation, *Ereignis* can also be said "to expropriate" itself such that expropriation too belongs to *Ereignis* as such. By this expropriation, *Ereignis* does not abandon itself—rather, it preserves what is its own or proper to it such that withdrawal belongs to "It" (GA 14: 28, 19/22–3, 15).

There are two further points upon which I would like to focus, points that concern Heidegger's descriptions of *Ereignis* presented here. I do this before turning to more critical observations regarding giving and the gift.

First, in Heidegger's description of *Ereignis*, the gift of presence, Being, which is the "property" [*Eigentum*] of *Ereignis* as appropriation or *taking* place, *vanishes* in *Ereignis*. Any "as" structure—and all that it implies—any "as" structure that would hold in tension a dynamic unity in difference, *disappears* in Heidegger's description of *Ereignis*. Thus, Heidegger tells us that in the expression "Being 'as' Ereignis," Being means simply letting-presence in *Ereignis*; where Time is concerned, "Time 'as' *Ereignis*" means simply extending-opening in *Ereignis*. We could put it this way in short: *Sein und Zeit ereignend im Ereignis*, or "Being and Time taking place in Taking Place." Ultimately, this means "only" *das Ereignis ereignet*, Taking Place takes place: "only" sheer eventing (GA 14: 29/24).

When we become attuned to sheer eventing in this way, we realize that the attempt "to overcome" metaphysics only reinforces metaphysics so that the proper thinking on this matter—or the proper way to expose ourselves to the matter itself, which can be realized in poetry and art, as well as in philosophy—calls thinking simply to cease all overcoming and to let metaphysics go its own way (GA 14: 30/24).

Second, Being and Time are gifts of giving, where the giving is qualified as sending/extending-opening. Given that "It" withdraws in favor of the gifts, given that "It" gives, given that *Ereignis* withdraws in expropriation as appropriation, given that the "as" structure disappears, what is the "status" of the gifts (if we are allowed to put it this way)? What "*happens*" to the gifts?

Heidegger assures us that although the withdrawal is peculiar to *Ereignis*, while we lose this tension of the "as," the gifts are *not ex-*

punged from the giving in the withdrawal.[20] The gifts, Heidegger reassures us, are *retained* in the self-withdrawing sending of giving. Being and Time are properties of *Ereignis* (in the sense of being proper to "It"); they belong to the "It gives"; accordingly, Being and Time, the gifts, *disappear in Ereignis*. Being and Time are appropriated in *Ereignis*: or Being and Time *take place* in Taking Place as expropriation.

In and of itself, and at least on a certain reading, Heidegger's descriptions may not be seen as problematic. After all, Heidegger is attempting to evoke the sheer unmotivated event of being released as letting-presence such that the gifts of Being and Time take place in *Ereignis*, in Taking Place. Although we can follow Heidegger to the extent that the gifts *take place in* Taking Place, although we might rest assured that the gifts are *retained* in the giving and not forsaken, although we can be reassured that the gifts *belong properly to Ereignis*, it is necessary, on my view, to make the following observation explicit: although the gifts are retained, for Heidegger, they are not retained *as* gifts.

These observations allow me to raise the following questions: If the gifts take place in *Ereignis*, if they are not expunged, does *Ereignis* take place in or as the gifts? Put still differently: Does the eventful giving accompany the gifts *as* gifts? However, nowhere in *Zeit und Sein* (in the explication of the retention of the gifts in the giving), nowhere in the comfort that the gifts are not lost, nowhere do we have a further recognition or even hint that the *giving is revealed in and takes It's place in the gifts*, in other words, that *Ereignis* takes place *as* gifts, or takes itself up *in* the gifts.

For Heidegger's part, interestingly, the gifts of Being and Time *do* qualify the happening in *Ereignis* when the "as" disappears. This is to say that *Ereignis, while impersonal, is not neutral* because "It" is not the same upon the delivery of the gifts of Being and Time. The "as" vanishes, but Being and Time retained in *Ereignis* means that *Ereignis* is qualified *according to the gifts*: Being colors *Ereignis* in the way of Being/sending ("*Anwesenlassen geschickt im Ereignen*"); Time colors *Ereignis* in the way of Time/extending-opening ("*Zeit gereicht im Ereignen*"). But Heidegger does not go so far as to say that *Ereignis*

---

20. GA 14 10/6: "Sein gehört als die Gabe dieses Es gibt in das Geben. Sein wird als Gabe nicht aus dem Geben abgestoßen." And GA 14: 13/9: "Jeweils einbehalten in der sich entziehenden Schickung wird das Sein mit seiner epochalen Wandlungsfülle dem Denken entborgen."

accompanies Being and is *revealed* in Being *as* Being, that *Ereignis accompanies* Time and is *revealed* in Time *as* Time.

Of course, one can appreciate Heidegger's sensitivity here: he is trying to face sheer eventing and to give heed to that indeterminacy and to that mystery. What occurs, occurs within *Ereignis*, and this insight seems to preclude his saying anything about *how Ereignis* occurs in the gifts. They are appropriated in *Ereignis*, but we can apparently say nothing about *Ereignis* in them. On this understanding, for Heidegger, the point would be precisely not to take responsibility for the sending or extending-opening because as Heidegger attempts to evoke it in another work, it is that "enigmatic region where there is nothing for which to be responsible."[21] For "Its" part, it is absolutely indifferent, sheer taking place.

The point would rather be *not to obscure the sheer eventing* or sheer "gifting" in whichever way the gift has been delivered over to itself, appropriated in the eventing. The gifts are no-thing. *Ereignis* is nothing, and our effort, the thinkers' effort (if it can be called that), is to step back to a more originary dimension of experience and *to reflect* (i.e., to think and to mirror) *Ereignis* taking place, to let "take place" without intrusion or getting in the way of the giving. Our thinking "task" would therefore reflect nonobtrusively, without memory, without anticipation, the "Taking-place" as it takes-place. Sheer eventing is sheer destining.

3. CRITICAL OBSERVATIONS: THE GIFTS AND RESPONSIBILITY

We have seemingly taken a few steps back, from beings to Being, from Being and Time as gifts to giving, from giving to the "It" as *Ereignis*. According to Heidegger, the gifts are not expurgated, but retained in *Ereignis*; Time and Being take place in Taking Place, disappearing as they send/extend-open. Sheer destining in this way admits decisively no point or motivation for responsibility.

For Heidegger, the forgetfulness of Being and machination that is occasioned by the withdrawal cannot be simply because of a deficit in human existence; rather, in a more primordial manner, "It gives" itself

21. Martin Heidegger, *Feldweg-Gespräche (1944/45)*, Gesamtausgabe 77, ed. Ingrid Schüssler, 2nd ed. (Frankfurt am Main: Vittorio Klostermann, 2007), 120. "Eine rätselhafte Gegend, wo es nichts zu verantworten gibt."

to be forgotten. Original forgetfulness would then be the veiling [*Verhüllung*] of the difference between Being and beings understood as concealment. This veiling "has in turn withdrawn itself from the beginning" such that forgetfulness is not a consequence of mere human thinking (or unthinking), *but must be somehow endemic to the withdrawal itself.* Machination is a sent forgetfulness rooted in the denial of the presencing of Being, as withholding the disclosure of *Ereignis.*[22] (This anticipates the discussion of forgetfulness in Chapter 3 concerning givenness in Michel Henry.)

But, to play on Heidegger's metaphors, do we not also need a step forward, completing the step back? On my view, not only do we have to recognize that the gifts are retained in the giving, as Heidegger recognizes; we also have to acknowledge that *giving accompanies its givenness in and as the gifts.* To put it in Heidegger's terms, I would insist that Time "takes place" *as* the revelation, *as* the extending-opening of *Ereignis*; Being "takes place" *as* the revelation, *as* the sending-presence of *Ereignis*. Recognizing this, or going this far, however, would be going too far for the position advocated by Heidegger because it would place his thinking into a radically different structure in a twofold sense.

First, if the "as" structure were to remain functional, *Ereignis*—in sustaining Being and Time *as* Being and Time, in sustaining them as gifts—would retain the tension of the revelatory gifts, Being and Time. Second, the sustaining-giving at this level would have to be qualified more radically—not as a sending or extending-opening—but more specifically as loving, as a unique *Ereignis* of difference, to play on Heidegger's terms. Eventful giving as loving in turn would qualify the impersonal "It" or *Ereignis* now as Lover-Loving Movement, becoming in and through loving; the gifts would be qualified as the "beloveds."

I am not simply replacing terms here (loving for giving, Lover for *Ereignis*, beloveds for gifts). There is a qualitative and decisive difference: Loving, by virtue of its very structure, "*cannot*" *withdraw, deny, or hold back*, such that infinite Loving "must" boundlessly accompany its "free," creative revelation (which is also a self-revelation) *as* and *in*

---

22. See Martin Heidegger, *Identität und Differenz* (1955–1957), Gesamtausgabe 11, ed. Friedrich-Wilhelm v. Herrmann (Frankfurt am Main: Vittorio Klostermann, 2006), 59. And see Arthur R. Luther, "Original Emergence in Heidegger and Nishida," *Philosophy Today* 26, no. 4/4 (1982): 345–56.

the beloved.[23] (For instance, in the movement of loving, I cannot anticipate an end to loving (e.g., "I will stop loving you in five years,"
etc.[24]). The taking place of that Loving is not merely "Being," or a
mode of being (Da-sein), but the "beloved," which is precisely the beloved as retaining and creatively originating the revelation of loving *as*
such. Where human beings are concerned, the loving is qualified personally such that the Lover is revealed as Person and the beloveds who
love as persons.

Loving holds or sustains the dynamic tension of Lover and beloved
in their difference (through the "event of difference," or rather, personal loving). More specifically, the Lover reveals itself through loving *as*
beloved. To be sure, it holds the beloved in loving, but the Lover also
accompanies the beloved in that revelation. Rather than expropriation
or simply appropriation, rather than denying, withholding, holding
back, I understand loving as "necessarily," infinitely accompanying its
own revelation, vigilant in its loving, as letting beloveds become what
or, in an inter-Personal and interpersonal nexus, *who* they are. The
individuals are let be, but in their uniqueness, without vigilant, overabundant loving somehow reducing them to radical immanence.[25]

We find such an experience articulated—not in the *paganism* of the
ancient Greeks, who for Heidegger already stood within Being and
hence did not have or need culture[26]—in the Abrahamic mystics: in the
experience of *baqa* or sustaining, in the experience of the sparks of
Holiness being contained in every shard of the broken vessels or the
Name being found in every name, or again where the "Father," "Mother," or "Parent" is given as and in the children, uniquely. It comes down
to being able to account for individuation, uniqueness in an interpersonal and inter-Personal nexus.

On this understanding, I would understand machination as problematic because of the over-accompanying Loving that is always somehow there because machination goes against the presence of person,
infinite and/or finite. It is not because of the withdrawal of giving or the
forgetfulness of Being, but to the violation of loving where infinite
Person and finite persons are concerned. The problem of machination is

---

23. See, for example, Max Scheler, *Vom Ewigen im Menschen*, Gesammelte Werke,
vol. 5, edited by Maria Scheler (Bern: Francke, 1954), 330–32.
24. See Steinbock, *Moral Emotions*, Chapters 4 and 7.
25. See Steinbock, *Phenomenology and Mysticism*. See Chapter 3 of this work on
Michel Henry.
26. Heidegger, GA 95: 322, 325–26; GA 96: 95, 125.

experienced most profoundly in this way, in the turning away from persistent Loving. This also means that the revelation of Loving is what is "normal," and it is machination that is "abnormal" because it takes place within the ongoing vigilance of Loving.[27] In short, characterizing the movement as the "withdrawal," "denial," "withholding" of *Ereignis*/giving constitutes a profound *misunderstanding* of our belonging-together, a misunderstanding that we can see has dramatic consequences for Heidegger.

One of the consequences is the following. For the Heidegger of the *Black Notebooks*, both the *matter* and *way* of our philosophizing "is *never* thinking about 'others'—the 'you'" (and even less so about the "I"), but uniquely about and for the origin of Being.[28] For Heidegger, it is not about the "others" in the sense of the plural, or about the other, the You, in the sense of singular uniqueness, or about Myself in the dynamic relational or vocational sense, or even about the "I-you" word pair, as in Martin Buber's thinking.[29]

But for the mystics of the Abrahamic "culture," for whom loving is central, and who also "retreat" and seek the "source" through the experience, God, the Holy, the Origin, or the Godhead is immediately and directly *connected to the love of neighbor or the stranger*. It is not possible within this structure to be comforted with or within the origin of Being/Beyng and to be unconcerned with the "You," "the other," or the I/Myself (where the latter is understood relationally). The so-called "religious" and the "moral" are inextricably and mutually bound, intertwining and delimiting, and for essential reasons.

To be sure, there are statements throughout Heidegger's works suggesting that he is sensitive to the issues of uniqueness or individuation. Indeed, in the *Black Notebooks*, he is also wary of succumbing to the intoxicating allure of the quantitative expressed in machination, and therefore of losing the sense of qualitative uniqueness. He gives an example: so that we do not become distracted from our "German" way, we should not assume that the killing of thousands is somehow worse than the killing of one person simply because the former is "more." The

---

27. For a clarification of the sense of "normal" and "abnormal" here, see Anthony J. Steinbock, *Home and Beyond: Generative Phenomenology after Husserl* (Evanston, IL: Northwestern University Press, 1995), section 3.

28. Heidegger, GA 94: 28: "Im Philosophieren *nie* an die 'Anderen'—an das 'Du' denken, aber ebensowenig an das 'Ich', einzig an und für den Ursprung des Seins—das gilt von Sache und Weg gleichermaßen."

29. Martin Buber, "Ich und Du," in *Das dialogische Prinzip* (Heidelberg: Lambert Schneider, 1965).

single individual is already the most! This could lead to the danger of supposing that killing fewer is better because it is a smaller quantity (GA 96: 237). Fine.

But without an interpersonal basis, how can we adjudicate this very qualitative dimension that Heidegger putatively evokes? According to Heidegger, if we ask "what" the human being is, we presuppose the human being as a human animal, and the implication is that we remain entrapped in machination's order of the undifferentiated organic, biological sphere, or treat the human being merely within anthropology. But, he asserts, when we ask the "who" question of the human being, we appropriately situate the human as the in-standing in the Truth of Beyng (GA 95: 322). The question for me is whether such a distinctiveness of a mode of being speaks decisively to the uniqueness of the individual concrete "being."

The problem is that his qualitative distinction is not "personal" and retreats from individuation in the interpersonal sphere to an individuation of the modality of the Da in relation to other modes of being. Although machination might result in assuming that murdering many is worse than murdering few because it is "fewer," how can the mere modal distinction of the "who" of the "Da" of Da-sein take a stand against not only the murder of one, but murdering many *just because* it "amounts to the same thing" as the murder of one?

Heidegger had the good sense to expunge that infamous line that I cited above from the *Question Concerning Technology* (a work, by the way, that was penned after the *Black Notebooks*), namely, that the motorized food industry is the same as the production of corpses in the gas chambers. Could this be a sign that he took seriously his distinction between the "what" and the "who"? Within the Jewish tradition, it is said that to save a life is to save a world. But this is based on the uniqueness of the person (e.g., within the context of loving-beloved).

For thinkers like Emmanuel Lévinas, indeed, the face of the Other is the trace of God, where the Other "teaches" the idea of Infinity; for thinkers like Max Scheler, the personal presence is exemplary of the Holy, of "Personal Loving." This absolute distinctiveness is not "because" of "God" or "the Holy" as if the only value of the other person were the latter. Precisely as "gifts," precisely as having their own integrity that each originates uniquely, persons are uniquely "who" they are, without deriving their value simply from the "Holy" or the "Giving."

But even here, it's not about the gift, but the interpersonal nexus in which it becomes meaningful at all.[30]

The point here is that one is immediately and directly responsible for the other person before I could choose to be responsible or not. This is what Lévinas calls *election*, not "sending/extending." It is not a matter of quibbling over terms, but the meaning that infuses them. An election before I could choose, which obligates me with responsibility and a new kind of freedom as binding me to another; an ante-memorial origin that accompanies His/Her revelation is not a sending/extending whose "origin" withdraws or denies in favor of the gift, and for which there is nothing to be responsible.[31]

If the giving accompanies the revelation in the gift, *as* the gift, then the integrity of the person/loving is given in each and every personal presence. There is a double demand and a double violation: moral and religious. Rather than withdrawal and forgetfulness, it concerns murder, on the one hand, and idolatry, on the other, and they are intertwined.[32] The inextricable double violation would at least provoke guilt (for what we have done), shame (for who we have become against who we most deeply are), and the possibility of repentance (turning to our deeper selves with others). It is no coincidence that we find in Jaspers a description of both a metaphysical guilt that is grounded in a solidarity

---

30. See Chapter 5.
31. See Emmanuel Lévinas, "Being Jewish," trans. Mary Beth Mader, *Continental Philosophy Review* 40 (2007): 209–10:

> The meaning of election, and of revelation understood as election, is not to be found in the injustice of a preference. It presupposes the relation of father to children in which each one is everything to the father without excluding the others from this privilege. Thus, Jewish election is not initially lived as pride or particularism. It is the very mystery of personhood. Against every attempt to understand the ego starting from a freedom, in a world without origin, the Jew offers to others, but already lives, the emotional schema of personhood as a son and as elected.
>
> In a new sense, then, to be created and to be a son is to be free. To exist as a creature is not to be crushed beneath adult responsibility. It is to refer in one's very facticity to someone who bears existence for you, who bears sin, who can forgive.
>
> Jewish existence is thus the fulfillment of the human condition as fact, personhood and freedom. And its entire originality consists in breaking with a world that is without origin and simply present.

32. See Steinbock, *Phenomenology and Mysticism*, esp. Chapters 6 and 8.

among all persons such that each person is co-responsible for every wrong and injustice in the world, and likewise a description of a moral guilt in which I am responsible as an individual for all that I do, within a loving struggle between persons in solidarity.[33]

Heidegger purposefully distances himself from "*an individuation in the moral-metaphysical sense of the 'person*'" (my emphasis). Instead, for him, it concerns the retrieval and taking over of the modal character of the "Da" [the "There" or "Here" of Da-sein] from its ontological anonymity with things and tools, as standing in the clearing (GA 96: 31). But for precisely this reason, in my view, Heidegger is still too far "this side" of specificity to provoke guilt, shame, repentance, and responsibility.[34] We lack the direct interpersonal encounter, the face-to-face or the person-to-person in which the other would be revealed and make us in awe, not of the source of Being or as the harbinger of a new beginning, but of the unique other and the unique "Myself" as beloved.

The "occurrence" of six million Jews gassed and tortured could not be a historical happening reducible to an anonymous *Machenschaft*; the mass murders in the gulags, the persecution of gays and lesbians, the institutionalization of racism and slavery is not an eventing for which there is nothing to be responsible, nothing for which to be guilty or ashamed, or nothing for which to repent. It is not particularly illuminating to assert as Heidegger does that there are slave markets in which the slaves themselves are often the biggest slave handlers—whether this be a veiled reference to our own place in machination, or an insensitive or misguided allusion to responsibility, another way of articulating his reprehensible contention (during the Shoah itself) that the Jews are or Jewry is the principle of their own/our own destruction, or the citation of mere historical fact (GA 95: 455). Without the context and movement of loving, and loving given irreducibly "in" the beloved, there is no responsibility, no shame, no guilt, no repentance; we have only sheer eventing, which can only be historicized.

This may seem unfair to Heidegger. Of course, for Heidegger, to attempt to think such specificity beyond metaphysics is illusory at best because we are not there yet. Rather than reinforcing it by trying to get beyond it, we have to let metaphysics be. For him, this cannot become a new ground of morality or a basis for religion and so on in part because

---

33. Karl Jaspers, *Die Schuldfrage: Ein Beitrage zur deutschen Frage* (Munich: Piper Verlag, 1947/1965). English translation, Karl Jaspers, *The Question of German Guilt*, trans. E. B. Ashton (New York: Fordham University Press, 2000).
34. See Steinbock, *Moral Emotions*.

the latter are still determined within Western metaphysics. What they would mean concretely beyond Western metaphysics is still open, and thus for him still vague.

Yet it is possible to pose one further question: Does overcoming metaphysics as not trying to overcome metaphysics, does getting beyond machination, mean that we need a different kind of *thinking*, a thoughtful speaking of the abyss of Beyng (e.g., Hölderlin, as the founder of decisive resoluteness)? Instead, do we not need to draw on the sphere that is most intimate to persons, namely, the emotions, which are other than reason and sensibility? Do we not need, more specifically, loving, or at least a deeper kind of *loving*? As important as they are, our only exemplars cannot be the "thinker" or the "poet," but the "lover," or the saint, the tzaddik, the friend of God.[35]

The basic problem in Heidegger is that he, philosophically for his own reasons, could not come to terms with uniqueness or singularity or individuation in an appropriate manner. By stark contrast, Viktor Frankl does: "This uniqueness and singleness which distinguishes each individual and gives a meaning to his existence has a bearing on creative work as much as it does on human love. When the impossibility of replacing a person is realized, it allows the responsibility which a man has for his existence and its continuance to appear in all its magnitude." He continues writing that one who becomes conscious of the responsibility that he or she bears toward a human being will never be able to throw away his or her life, and knowing this "why" of his or her existence, he or she is able to bear almost any "how."[36]

Let me finally hasten to add that this does not mean that Heidegger's work is meaningless; it does not mean that it is contaminated; it does not mean that it is fascist. The philosophical difficulties are not just with Heidegger alone. In fact, Heidegger is at least confronting the problem in a profound, reflective way—which is more than most of us do. We can still sort through those insights that are helpful for us overall. But his "matter and way" are all the more misleading because of his depth. What is called for when confronting the stranglehold of calculating managerial technologies or machination is not a novel paganism of thinking, but a rehabilitation, a reclamation of the emotional sphere of human persons, and in particular, the interpersonal emotions,

---

35. See Steinbock, *Phenomenology and Mysticism*.
36. Viktor E. Frankl, *Man's Search for Meaning*, trans. Ilse Lasch (Boston: Beacon Press, 2006), 79–80.

which give us novel ways of freedom, critique, normativity, and specifically, a deeper sense of person.

If this were the case, then as I have suggested above, eventful giving, Taking Place taking place, would be qualified through loving. The impersonal "It" or *Ereignis*, would be revealed in a concrete inter-Personal relation now as Lover-Loving movement. The "gifts" would be qualified interpersonally as the "beloveds" in which gifts of a different sort would be received in interpersonal relations. Withdrawal would not be peculiar to "Being," but enacted as a refusal—ultimately of loving. The matter of "overcoming"—if it would still be expressed like that—would not be of forgetfulness, but of idolatry in a religious register, or pride, in a moral/interpersonal register.

The matters encountered above, in particular, the matters of giving and the gift are not just problems for ontology, metaphysics, nonmetaphysics, or "eventing." They are issues that emerge within phenomenology and even explicitly within religious discourse. In fact, in some ways they are formulated in different terms, but with equal import and consequence in the work of Michel Henry. A phenomenologist and explicitly religious thinker, Henry deals with the matter of giving and givenness in a way that can be read along the axis of the Heideggerian problem of forgetfulness. It is to this problem, formulated in phenomenological and religious terminology, that I now turn.[37]

---

37. A different version of this chapter was published in *Gatherings: The Heidegger Circle Annual* 5 (2015), 50–76, as "Heidegger, Machination, and the Jews: The Problem of the Gift."

Chapter 3

Overcoming Forgetfulness

Henry's Challenge of Self-Givenness

The problem of forgetfulness figures diversely in twentieth-century thought, especially in the thought that characterizes itself as phenomenological. For Edmund Husserl, forgetfulness was initially formulated as the problem of the natural attitude, the style of comportment by which one takes for granted the givenness of sense, literally presupposing the being of the world and the being of the self. This forgetfulness was later clarified by Husserl as the forgetfulness of the Earth as "Boden"—the "ground" or "footing" of all aesthetic, corporeal sense—as well as the forgetfulness of the world as horizon, functioning as the condition of historical determinations: both of which (Earth and world) withdraw from all forms of objectivating activity. In short, forgetfulness was expressed as the forgetfulness of the "lifeworld," constituting a crisis in the developmental integrity of reason and the realization of humanity.

Although Heidegger did not explicitly appropriate the terminology of crisis, he did formulate a related problem of forgetfulness, one that is explicitly "ontological." Forgetfulness is "ontological" in at least three senses. First, forgetfulness is the forgetfulness of Being, which for Heidegger means Dasein's forgetfulness of "ontological difference," the difference between Being and beings.[1] This forgetfulness is coeval

---

1. See Martin Heidegger, *Holzwege*, 6th ed. (Frankfurt am Main: Klostermann, 1980), 360.

49

with the emergence of "metaphysics." Second, forgetfulness is ontological in the sense that it is essential to metaphysics and characteristic of
Western thought itself. Third, forgetfulness is thrown in the sense that
it is given by the withdrawal of Being or the "It" that gives in favor of
the given gifts.

The work of Michel Henry is heir to this phenomenological tradition, not simply because he employs key phenomenological notions or
because he provides us with insightful and rich meditations on the
works of earlier phenomenologists, but because he inquires into the
very meaning of human being, connects it in his own way to the problem of givenness and to the gift by which Life gives itself to itself. This
chapter examines Michel Henry's formulation of the problem of forgetfulness as emerges from his phenomenology of giving and the gift of
Life.

After a few initial remarks of clarification, I introduce Henry's concepts of immanence and transcendence (1) and then elaborate upon the
problem of forgetfulness as ontological monism, or a myopic restriction of givenness (2). Going from his earlier articulation of the matter
in terms of what we can call ontological, existential, and historical
modes of forgetfulness, I turn to one of his subsequent works where
Henry understands forgetfulness as the forgetfulness of the condition of
Sonship (3). I then address the ways in which Henry portrays a possible
overcoming of forgetfulness through a "second birth" and the salvific
role of "doing" in relation to the gift of Life (4). I conclude with some
critical reflections on the relation between forgetfulness and idolatry,
proposing the possibility of doing-acts of mercy and the intertwining of
the religious and moral spheres of experience.

INTRODUCTION

It is important to note at the outset that the founding insight for Henry—an insight that lends a strict internal coherence to his works—is not
and cannot be that of forgetfulness, but immanence.[2] I say this because

---

2. For a study devoted to the concept of immanence in Henry, see Sébastien Laou-
reux, *L'immanence à la limite: recherches sur la phénoménologie de Michel Henry*
(Paris: Les Éditions du Cerf, 2005). See also Jeffrey Hanson and Michael R. Kelly, "The
Idea of Phenomenology: Immanence, Givenness and Reflection," in *Michel Henry: The
Affects of Thought*, ed. Jeffrey Hanson and Michael R. Kelly (New York: Bloomsbury,
2014), 62–84.

it is only within the context of immanence that forgetfulness can emerge as a problem.

Philosophically, the insight into immanence is grounded in a reflective point of departure that can be called "transcendental." It is transcendental in at least three senses: First, Henry is attuned to modes of givenness, to the how of givenness, and not simply into what something is. Second, his inquiry focuses on the very being of the beings given; that is, he attempts to elucidate the ontological or essential structure of reality. Third—and this is peculiar to all Modern thinkers, from Machiavelli to Husserl (to Husserl, at least)—Henry gives an account of transcendence in terms of immanence. But whereas the Modern tendency is to relocate transcendence within immanence, Henry does not take transcendence to be immanent to immanence because immanence as such must essentially exclude transcendence. This has to do with the very reality of the absolute essence and how it receives itself (i.e., the how of its reception). This is why Henry's ontological/phenomenological descriptions are rich with religious and moral implications, and vice versa, and why he does not hesitate to use the terms like "phenomenological" within his characterization of the Divine essence, Life, God, and so on. His earlier and later works reveal the same essence.

The talk of immanence will undoubtedly provoke an uneasiness in those of us who are particularly attentive to notions like "Transcendence" or "Exteriority," notions that already abound in contemporary thought. Indeed, one would be tempted to say that such an emphasis on immanence would constitute its own type of forgetfulness, the forgetfulness of Transcendence, which in its own way can lead to totalization or totality—to employ the terminology of Emmanuel Lévinas. But to launch into a facile critique of Henry merely because we are habituated to "Transcendence" or the "Other" would be to misunderstand the significance and profound import of Henry's insights. It would be expressive of the problem exemplified at different stages throughout the history of philosophy identified by Henry himself: we have forgotten what constitutes the utmost possibility of transcendence itself, namely, immanence, and the depreciation of the essential meaning of immanence can arise only through such a forgetfulness.[3] Immanence and transcendence are not juxtaposed or correlative; rather, immanence according to

---

3. Michel Henry, *L'essence de la manifestation*, 2nd ed. (Paris: PUF, 1990), 324. Michel Henry, *The Essence of Manifestation*, trans. Girard Etzkorn (The Hague: Martinus Nijhoff, 1973), 261.

Henry is the essence of transcendence, and immanence, as Unity or an original internal coherence, receives transcendence and makes it possible.[4]

But if the founding insight of Henry's thought is immanence, it is no less true that forgetfulness functions as the clue to immanence, and it is along the bias of forgetfulness that we can understand the problem of givenness in Henry's works. The problem of forgetfulness is formulated by Henry both in his early monumental work, *L'essence de la manifestation* (1963), and his work that comes almost a quarter century after, *C'est moi la vérité* (1996).[5] In the former case, the problem is formulated as a forgetfulness of the original essence of revelation (immanence, affectivity, Life), and in the latter is explicated as the forgetfulness of our human condition as "Sons of God" and as "Sons among the Son." In the former, he articulates a phenomenology of self-affection; in the latter this becomes explicit as a phenomenology of the self-generation of Divine Life.

Although these two works, separated by more than three decades, do share the same internal structure, if they can be cast as different in some significant manner, it is because *I Am the Truth* is able to take more seriously the premises of *Essence* with respect to concepts such as immanence, revelation, the essence, Life, self-affection, and so on. For Henry, this does not vitiate the former's phenomenological character, but only reinforces it. In fact, a significant difference between the two can be seen in the way in which *I Am the Truth* gives a more explicit and tenable response (explicit and tenable, that is, within the framework of Henry's problematic) to how overcoming forgetfulness is possible.

The invocation of forgetfulness, so prominent within the phenomenological tradition, brings with it a certain series of questions. If we are able to understand the nature of this forgetfulness that plagues our existence in the lifeworld, our understanding of Being, our relation with the Holy as Person, or in Henry's terms, our relation to "essence" or to the self-generation of absolute Life, we must also ask whether it is possible to overcome this forgetfulness. If it is not, why not? If it is possible, how and to what extent? Is this forgetfulness itself given as part of giving itself? Can overcoming it be accomplished through re-

---

4.   Henry, *L'essence*, 333; Henry, *Essence*, 268.
5.   Michel Henry, *C'est moi la vérité: pour une philosophie du christianisme* (Paris: Seuil, 1996). Michel Henry, *I Am the Truth: Toward a Philosophy of Christianity*, trans. Susan Emanuel (Stanford, CA: Stanford University Press, 2002).

flection? Does it require a special type of remembering or thinking? Does it demand an ethical or a religious life? What does the problem of forgetfulness tell us about ourselves in an ontological, existential, religious, or moral register? Is the language of forgetfulness ultimately appropriate for evoking this situation, or should it be reformulated? And if so, how?

Henry has a distinctive take on these phenomenological issues, explicitly and implicitly. Let me explicate the problem of forgetfulness as suggested in *Essence of Manifestation* and then turn to the problem as formulated in *I Am the Truth*. I conclude with critical reflections on the problem of forgetfulness and treat the implications it has for action, the givenness of transcendence, individuation, and the relation between the individual person and absolute Life.

1. TRANSCENDENCE AND IMMANENCE

Forgetfulness is a forgetfulness of the essence or immanence. To understand how forgetfulness could be expressed as a forgetfulness of immanence, it will be helpful to describe two different modes of givenness. By virtue of Henry's starting point, which is actually the "essence," Henry can speak of givenness in terms of receptivity. There are two ways in which the essence can receive, two modes of receptivity: manifestation and revelation. Let me explain these modes of givenness by explicating the related terms, transcendence and immanence.

Transcendence

Transcendence is an active power of disposition by which individuals surpass themselves in the world toward some particular perceptual or epistemological theme or themes (be they understood as perceptual objects, images, or ideational representations) having a system of referential implications or horizon.[6] In the classical terminology of phenomenology, consciousness is always consciousness of something, and through the intentional structure, this something is situated in a context. Precisely through this movement of transcendence, even the horizontal

---

6. See Henry, *L'essence*, 349; Henry, *Essence*, 281: "Where there is no transcendence, there is neither horizon nor world. Far from being a universal structure of all manifestation, and consequently, of constituting the essence of the latter, the horizon of the world is, on the contrary, excluded from this essence considered in itself." And see Husserl, *Analyses*, Part 2, "Self-Giving in Perception."

context—when directed toward it—gets determined as theme. Something given in this way exerts a more or less intensive allure, becoming more or less affective, superimposing itself on others to stand out and to be perceived explicitly. Under the rubric of transcendence, we understand not only the active projection of self in exteriority, but the givenness of the object, soliciting the subject for its constitution, in short, everything that would fit under the Husserlian rubric of "passive synthesis": the structure of retention and protention; syntheses of association; and the exertion of an affection on the perceiver, self-temporalization, and so on.[7]

Something is given through transcendence in the mode of manifestation. Peculiar to manifestation is a disclosing and a concealing. For this reason, manifestation means hiddenness, or again, it means that something differs from the appearance that indicates what it is in itself, its essence.[8] To adapt a phrase from Husserl, one could say that transcendence is a constant pretension to accomplish something that by its very nature it is not in a position to accomplish, namely, the complete givenness of the object as such, because the whole object appears only at a distance through perspectives or profiles as the "how" of its determination.

But can transcendence account for its own condition, or put differently, can the very essence of manifestation, which does not appear as an object in the world, become an object of manifestation?

Transcendence, according to Henry, does not have the power to disclose the essence, or more exactly, precisely because transcendence is the power to disclose, the essence cannot *be given* as manifest because this would putatively make of transcendence an object. In terms of transcendence, the essence of transcendence necessarily remains hidden. The essence escapes its thematization or determination as an object to be given precisely in its movement toward it. Thus, forgetfulness of the essence is for Henry essential to the movement of transcendence that implicitly tries to contain the "source" of finite, determined, historical structures within those finite, determined, historical structures.

7.　See Husserl, Analyses, Part 2, Division 3.
8.　Henry, *L'essence*, 297; Henry, *Essence*, 240.

Immanence

Transcendence is the active power of going beyond itself, positing sense and being affected by aspects of the world that become prominent. Transcendence, however, cannot receive itself by virtue of transcendence. If transcendence were its own condition, this condition would always go beyond itself in exteriority and could never receive itself. The condition for transcendence to relate itself to something other than itself, the condition for transcendence to be affected by something in the world by the givenness or pregivenness of the object, essentially has to exclude the structure of transcendence. This condition of transcendence, which is the *givenness of transcendence to itself*, is what Henry calls immanence.

Immanence is literally "in itself," having no gaps, without temporal distance, and does not surpass itself; it is radical interiority, plenitude, unity, complete self-presence.[9] Being the original ontological possibility of transcendence itself, immanence is thus "transcendental."[10] Accordingly, the fact that transcendence is excluded from the structure of immanence allows transcendence to be given to itself. "It is because it maintains itself outside exteriority that the essence can open itself to exteriority, it is because it does not show itself in it that it is the condition of exteriority."[11]

Whereas manifestation is the way in which transcendence has access to the object, transcendence cannot receive itself in manifestation. The self-givenness of transcendence, as the condition of the possibility of the object being given, is given in an entirely different way, what Henry calls *revelation*. An object can only be given to transcendence, "manifest," if transcendence is already given to itself, and transcendence can only be given to itself not in the mode of manifestation, but on the basis of immanence in the mode of revelation.

Self-givenness in the mode of revelation, according to Henry, is immediate, direct, absolute self-givenness, not chiasmatic, noncoincidental, as in Merleau-Ponty, not ecstatic as in Heidegger, not self-

---

9. See Henry, *L'essence*, 356; Henry, *Essence*, 286: *"It pertains to the essence which gives itself to itself in unity and as this very unity to give itself to itself in the totality of its reality. . . . Unity designates the original mode of presence of the essence to itself"* (translation slightly modified). And see *L'essence*, 279–80, 358; *Essence*, 226–27, 287. See also Dan Zahavi, "Michel Henry and the Phenomenology of the Invisible," *Continental Philosophy Review* 32, no. 3 (1999): 223–40.

10. Henry, *L'essence*, 308–309, 323, 349; Henry, *Essence*, 260, 248–49, 281.

11. Henry, *L'essence*, 498; Henry, *Essence*, 396.

temporalizing as in Husserl, not mediated as in Hegel. The movement of transcendence is given to itself through the essence of manifestation, in the mode of revelation, in pure nonobjectivating passivity. Passivity is the ontological determination of revelation.[12] Immanence as Life is nonintentional and is self-given, revealed in a pathetic self-affection as in an immediate identity of, for example, sorrow and the experience of sorrow, joy and the experience of joy. Because immanence is not active or powerful in the manner of transcendence, projecting itself outward as the power to disclose, not only is it revealed in its innermost nature as passive and impotent, but I literally can do nothing about it. As transcendence, I simply take it up; I am simply given to myself, *receive the gift of myself to myself as a projection beyond myself.*

The receptivity operative in transcendence is the power of transcendence to be affected by the world. The passive receptivity peculiar to immanence is the "impotence" of receiving itself. This immediate, nonobjectivating, passive self-givenness peculiar to revelation, which is the possibility of the essence receiving itself, is what Henry understands as self-affection or affectivity. In and through transcendence, which projects a figure/horizon and is affected by it, transcendence is already self-affected, given immediately to itself; self-affection or affectivity is the condition for something exercising an affection on me. In turn, the noninterpolative self-affection of the self, which is the revelation of the self to the self, is the self-affection of the essence.

On the one hand, the self-affection of transcendence is the way in which the essence affects itself; affectivity is the fundamental way in which the essence receives itself, reuniting itself to itself. On the other hand, the essence affecting itself is the self-affection of transcendence and enables transcendence to be affected by the world and receive it in modes of manifestation. For Henry, self-affection in immanence is simultaneously the accomplishment of Life (God, the Essence), the revelation of Life to itself.[13] This is why revelation for him, not manifestation, is the most profound and most fundamental mode of givenness.

This is where we have arrived: self-givenness as self-affection is the condition of the givenness of the world, but my self-affection is also the self-affection of Life affecting itself. There is no manifestation of the world and also no revelation of the human being to itself without the simultaneous revelation of the Absolute.[14]

---

12. Henry, *L'essence*, 366; Henry, *Essence*, 294.
13. Henry, *L'essence*, 367; Henry, *Essence*, 295.
14. Henry, *L'essence*, 382–83; Henry, *Essence*, 307.

But if there is absolute self-presence, if there is no givenness or manifestation of objects without the revelation of the essence of manifestation, if there is no self-givenness, no revelation of the self without the self-revelation of absolute Life, how is it possible to become forgetful of the Essence? To respond to this question, it is necessary to understand the nature of forgetfulness.

At the very core of the problem of forgetfulness are issues that have far-ranging implications, not just for epistemology and ontology, but for the moral and religious life. Can the forgetfulness of absolute essence be overcome by remembering? Is forgetfulness given, a gift, and so, endemic to who we are such that there is no escape from it? Can acting in a certain way overcome forgetfulness, and to what extent are we empowered to do so? If transcendence is the active power to accomplish things in the world, is our "power" our condemnation to forgetfulness? Can this forgetfulness be made explicit to consciousness, and if so, how would this recognition differ from the transcendence of thought?

Henry's early work, *Essence*, provides a perspective on these questions, even though it does not fully resolve them—a perspective that arises in a more forceful manner in his *I Am the Truth*. Let me begin with the former to sketch the formulation and status of forgetfulness and then point to its reformulation in the latter.

2. FORGETFULNESS AS ONTOLOGICAL MONISM

The following distinctions I make concerning the concept of forgetfulness are not explicit in Henry's work; still, it is possible to find at least three senses implicit in *Essence*, one that can be called "ontological," one that can be called "existential," and one that can be called "historical." All of these are grounded, further, in what can be termed an "ontological hiddenness." After explaining the later, which is the ground of forgetfulness, I address the motivations for speaking of ontological, existential, and historical modes of forgetfulness. This will yield to a discussion of forgetfulness in the context of *I Am the Truth*.

Ontological Hiddenness

Immanence maintains itself in itself and does not disclose itself in exteriority, in the world. In this respect, it is alien to transcendence, to thought, to intentionality. Rather than this being a tragedy, the very exclusion of transcendence from immanence and the inaccessibility of immanence to transcendence (because immanence cannot in principle become manifest) *allow transcendence to be given to itself.* But precisely because immanence does not manifest itself in exteriority and in the phenomenality proper to it, immanence can never become objective, and this is what determines it as "hiddenness."[15] In a discussion of Merleau-Ponty, Henry writes: "It is because the foundation of exteriority maintains itself outside exteriority and does not manifest itself in it that consciousness wherein the foundation resides is said to be 'obscure' and not to show itself."[16] This obscurity or hiddenness, which is an essential hiddenness from transcendence, from manifestation, constitutes the very Being of the Absolute for Henry. One could say, in fact, hiddenness of the Absolute is an absolute hiddenness to thought.

Thus, the hiding of the essence is not related to the failure of thought, but to the essence itself, to the ontological structure of reality.[17] This is why, in his discussion of Meister Eckhart, Henry asserts that Being-hidden of the Divine essence is a name for immanence.[18] The essence remains hidden because in its modesty, it maintains itself outside the world and in no way appears in it. "Being-hidden characterizes the essence and belongs to it by virtue of its internal structure." It essentially affects this structure, which is precisely immanence as such. For Henry, then, immanence constitutes what is most interior to the Absolute itself, its essence.[19]

Granted, then, that there is an ontological hiddenness, the thorny issue becomes how forgetfulness is related to this hiddenness and how this relation qualifies forgetfulness. The response to this issue will also color the response concerning what, if anything, can be done about forgetfulness.

Ontological Forgetfulness

There is a certain textual motivation for interpreting forgetfulness as ontological. For example, there are explicit assertions in the context of Heidegger's thought that describe forgetfulness as both ontological and fundamental.[20] More importantly, however, are the formulations where

---

15.   Henry, *L'essence*, 382–83; Henry, *Essence*, 307.
16.   Henry, *L'essence*, 490; Henry, *Essence*, 389.
17.   Henry, *L'essence*, 478; Henry, *Essence*, 379.
18.   Henry, *L'essence*, 482; Henry, *Essence*, 382.
19.   Henry, *L'essence*, 481; Henry, *Essence*, 382.
20.   Henry, *L'essence*, 483; Henry, *Essence*, 383.

Henry writes as if the hiddenness peculiar to immanence determines a forgetfulness. Accordingly, one could express the emergence of forgetfulness this way: Because there is in immanence something opaque and its peculiar essence hides itself, thought therefore falls into forgetfulness, and this forgetfulness becomes the forgetfulness of its own essence by thought itself.[21] Such an ontological forgetfulness receives its determination from the perspective of immanence.

Existential Forgetfulness

Existential forgetfulness is really just a further elaboration of ontological forgetfulness, the flip side of it, as it were. It receives its determination from the perspective of transcendence. I call this forgetfulness an "existential" one because this forgetfulness is structured according to existence as transcendence, and existence, as we will see, mundane human existence, can do nothing else but transcend in perception and in thought, which is to say, can lose itself only in the world and forget immanence. Because thought is transcendence and aims at something outside the self, because it is in principle in the world, and because it cannot in principle achieve the essence that maintains itself outside exteriority, thought is condemned from the outset to forget immanence.[22]

Existential forgetfulness, then, is an elaboration of ontological forgetfulness in the sense that existence as transcendence lives in intentional acts. Accordingly, it can also attempt to recuperate what is always already forgotten through another intentional act, namely, remembering. Through remembering, an object gets constituted as such with a temporal density not available on the anonymous level of experience. Remembering attempts to overcome forgetfulness by recapturing what was forgotten and making it present again, representing it. Existential forgetfulness can be further qualified as a genetic forgetfulness because it belongs to the structure of intentional lived-experience as temporalizing.

The catch is that remembering still has the structure of transcendence and by its nature, would have to make of immanence an intentional, thematic object; hence, the attempt to remember would only redouble the problem of forgetfulness: re-membering still remains in

21. Henry, *L'essence*, 491–92; Henry, *Essence*, 390.
22. Henry, *L'essence*, 486; Henry, *Essence*, 386.

the forgetfulness of the essence.[23] Not only does this remembering intrinsically fail to eliminate the opaqueness of essence; it can only push it back further.[24] It pushes it back further because with respect to original immanence, "re-membering" just repeats the forgetfulness of naïve consciousness, producing an absolute forgetfulness. "*Thus, in thought, the forgetfulness of the essence cannot change itself into its contrary, because its contrary is rather identical to it.*"[25] This is why Henry writes that forgetfulness appears at the very core of the thought that achieves it; the very definition of existence as escape from self (transcendence) implies what it denies, namely, immanence as its presupposition.[26]

I have attempted to distinguish two types of forgetfulness governed by the essence of transcendence, which is immanence. I proceed now to a third understanding that can be characterized not as ontological or as existential, but as historical. Although Henry does not speak in this way, the historical sense of forgetfulness implies an active occlusion, omission, denial, or restriction for which we are responsible, and in this sense is creative. One could then describe motivations for the omission of immanence without these motivations amounting to a necessary denial of immanence. Rather than being a necessary perdition, one would still have the possibility here—not of recognizing or remembering—but of living ontological hiddenness as mystery.

Historical Forgetfulness

This final mode of forgetfulness that I call historical forgetfulness entails direct responsibility. In this case, one would not be condemned "to forget" ontological hiddenness. It would, however, surface through the creative (willful or not) restriction of all possible types of experience to one sole type of experience: the experience of transcendence in manifestation. This forgetfulness is what Henry calls "ontological monism."

Ontological monism is the restriction of givenness to one type of givenness. However, seen from the perspective of immanent revelation, this restriction is really the attempt to determine the essence revealed according to manifest givenness, to make immanence conform to the gestures of transcendence, thus in principle reducing revelation to man-

---

23. Henry, *L'essence*, 493; Henry, *Essence*, 392.
24. Henry, *L'essence*, 491–92; Henry, *Essence*, 390.
25. Henry, *L'essence*, 486; Henry, *Essence*, 385.
26. Henry, *L'essence*, 492; Henry, *Essence*, 390–91.

ifestation, immanence to transcendence, thereby suppressing Life. Rather than being given from the start, ontological monism would have to be understood as a creative elaboration of ontological hiddenness.

Accordingly, if it is possible to surmount this kind of forgetfulness, then what is overcome is not ontological hiddenness, the essential recusion of immanence from transcendence (for this would result in only a new type of forgetfulness), but ontological monism. In other words, the so-called overcoming could not have the nature of transcendence for him, but would itself have to be nonintentional, nontranscendent, nonworldly, and in this sense forgetful of transcendence itself! One hint in this direction provided by Henry (provisionally, anyway) is that ontological monism (or historical forgetfulness) can be challenged by no longer "denying" immanence as the essence of transcendence. Ontological hiddenness is no longer purposively subjected to transcendence, but is realized as not being able to be realized through transcendence, as what makes forgetfulness possible. According to Henry, immanence is presupposed by a philosophy of existence, and it, immanence, is what makes this forgetfulness possible. His attempt is to give a positive determination of immanence and to take the obscurity of existence itself as the theme of a philosophy of existence.[27]

A host of questions arise now. How is this thinking that can make ontological hiddenness thematic different from the thought that is an elaboration of existence as transcendence and thus lives in intentional acts? How can philosophy be in the position of no longer denying immanence if it is expressive of transcendence that necessarily forgets immanence? What kind of philosophical reflection would this be? One might be tempted to explain it in terms of the "radical reflection" of Merleau-Ponty's *Phénoménologie de la perception*, a reflection that is sensitive to what he calls "ontological contingency." Or again, one could compare it to Merleau-Ponty's later "hyper-reflection" articulated in his *Le visible et l'invisible*. Or perhaps it is a matter of taking a precarious step outside of/inside of metaphysics, becoming attuned to ontological difference. Can it be achieved through so-called deconstructive means suggested either by Heidegger or Derrida?

---

27. Henry, *L'essence*, 494; Henry, *Essence*, 392–93: "That such obscurity should be that of the essence and constitute its most notable phenomenological characteristic, that the latter, moreover, is understood in its explicit opposition to the light of exteriority identified with the light of consciousness, becomes apparent to thought, which thinks all things, beginning with the essence."

Henry's point cannot be that immanence remains hidden, for this would be to interpret immanence from transcendence, but that immanence is given in a *mode that is entirely different from manifestation, namely, revelation.* So although Henry does express the nonforgetfulness of the essence in terms of thinking, he does point to a different avenue. He does this by suggesting that universal phenomenological ontology, which clarifies the horizon considered as an absolute essence, can become conscious of the basic obscurity that in principle belongs to the essence, "not for the purpose of surmounting it, it is true, but in order to live it as such, in mystery."[28]

Ontological obscurity cannot be overcome through transcendence, or rather, the attempt to do so would result precisely in forgetfulness. For the self-revelation of the essence *does not give itself in the mode of manifestation.* But because there is a revelation of immanence other than manifestation, it can be given in the mode of being "lived" passively immanently, as mystery. Living the essence immanently means being united (immanently) with the essence.[29]

If it is not possible to challenge forgetfulness through transcendence, Henry does suggest how it is possible to overcome forgetfulness, and thereby live the mystery as such, namely, *through ethical comportment.* This suggestion comes to the fore in his discussion of Echkart in *Essence.* This process of overcoming forgetfulness takes place through a "reduction" of sorts, though here the reduction is not an epistemological reduction; it is rather a transcendental/ethical one that is carried out in a different form of bracketing, living the "transcendental attitude" by renouncing the world through humility and poverty. Such a renouncing is the condition of union, if union is even to be possible, and it is bound to an "ethics" for its realization. The thought of Eckhart is edifying for Henry and expresses itself in preaching "because it aims at a transformation of existence and only after this will existence truly be united to God."[30]

Humility and poverty serve to dispose oneself to the essence because they are the processes by which one detaches him- or herself from everything that is not the essence; humility and poverty cooperate with God by renouncing all activity (i.e., all transcendence) and this, it must be emphasized, is primarily an ethical project and not a theoretical one. Indeed, one could go so far as to say that for Henry, humility and

---

28.   Henry, *L'essence*, 23; Henry, *Essence*, 18.
29.   Henry, *L'essence*, 407; Henry, *Essence*, 327.
30.   Henry, *L'essence*, 389–90; Henry, *Essence*, 312–13.

poverty are nonintentional, nonmanifest, nontranscendent ways of recovering immanence and overcoming forgetfulness.

Because the absolute is thought of by Eckhart as starting with the exclusion of otherness, humility and poverty serve to liberate the essential in the sense of casting out everything worldly: images, forms, representations, unreality, and so on. To be freed of images, to be in "union" with the absolute, is to realize the conditions that define the internal structure of the absolute. Henry concludes that this means to reject the ontological process in which being phenomenalizes itself as an "image" or "mediation"—that which in monism presents itself as the presupposition for all possible manifestation.[31] Seeing philosophically/ontologically is dependent upon a certain way of living because humility and poverty allow one to rediscover what already was or to reunite the human being and God because they liberate the essence; thus, they do not lead to a simple modification of human existence, but bring it to light in its essence.[32]

The suggestion that forgetfulness can be overcome through humility and poverty receives its fullest expression in the sections of *L'essence* devoted to Eckhart and point toward the process of living an ethical life as a way of being reunited with the essence, living ontological hiddenness as mystery. Let me suggest at the outset, however, that Henry's invocation of Meister Eckhart—which is more than an invocation because it is really the insight guiding the work as a whole—points in a different direction, in the direction of an ethical life as a way of overcoming forgetfulness.[33] But although there are gestures in this direction, it must also be said that the moral and religious implications of this work, *Essence*, remain implicit, especially in comparison to Henry's more recent work, *I Am the Truth*. It is here that Henry takes a stand that places the problem of forgetfulness more squarely in the

---

31. Henry, *L'essence*, 399; Henry, *Essence*, 320; translation slightly modified. "Because they accomplish the retreat from everything which is not the essence, humility and poverty lay bear the structure of the essence. . . . To lay bare the structure of the essence consists not merely in taking away that which covers it; it means still more to penetrate into it, to make it appear for what it is. Thus, the ontological task thought of under the concepts of humility and poverty is accomplished; their meaning is not merely to liberate the essence, they determine its internal structure." Henry, *L'essence*, 392; Henry, *Essence*, 314; translation slightly modified. See also Henry, *L'essence*, 405; Henry, *Essence*, 324–25.

32. Henry, *L'essence*, 394–95; Henry, *Essence*, 316–17.

33. See Natalie Depraz, "Seeking a Phenomenological Metaphysics: Henry's Reference to Meister Eckhart," trans. Gregory B. Sadler, in *The Philosophy of Michel Henry*, ed. Anthony J. Steinbock, *Continental Philosophy Review* 32 (1999): 303–24.

religious and ethical context of a phenomenological undertaking. It is to the depiction of the phenomenon of forgetfulness within this context that I now turn.

3. FORGETFULNESS OF THE CONDITION OF SONSHIP

Overcoming forgetfulness gets specified in *I Am the Truth* as taking place from absolute Life (not from the ego) and as a matter of both ethics and salvation. To situate the problem of forgetfulness, let me make the following preliminary remarks regarding Henry's understanding of human being.

Both the "common sense" and Modern scientific understanding of human being, contends Henry, have missed what it means to be human (and in this way we have become forgetful, if not "lost"). In the former case, the human being is grasped as a creature of the world, an animal endowed with reason; in the latter, Modern science has taken the human being to be part of the material universe, reduced in the final analysis to physico-chemical elements, in this respect a being essentially of objective reality.[34] It was only with the insights of Christianity, he asserts, that human nature has been grasped most profoundly.[35] In God and through Christ, the human being is not a "creature" of the world, not a part of the material universe to be objectively determined, but given to itself in and of absolute Life. According to the insights of Christianity, writes Henry, human beings are given to themselves as Sons in the Son because Christ is the primordial Son in the self-generation of God the Father. What distinguishes Christ as Son from human beings as Sons of God in the Son is that the former is identified with God in interior reciprocity: Christ cannot forget his identity with the Divine Life, whereas for the latter, the forgetfulness of this condition is not only possible; it is necessary, as we will see, rupturing our identity with God and requiring Christ's intercession.

This insight into the nature of human beings as Sons of God in the Son immediately qualifies the other definitions of human being (the commonsense and the scientific) as inverted in the sense of worldly, mundane, secular. The latter have understood human beings merely in

---

34. Henry, *C'est moi la vérité*, 120 ff.; Henry, *I Am the Truth*, 94 ff.
35. See also Rudolf Bernet, "Christianity and Philosophy," in *The Philosophy of Michel Henry*, ed. Anthony J. Steinbock, *Continental Philosophy Review* 32, no. 3 (1999): 325–42.

terms of transcendence, but not in terms of the essence of transcendence, namely, as revealed immanence.

Here, we revisit the questions posed earlier, but now in a new form: If human beings are intrinsically, essentially the Sons of God, and more specifically, the Sons of God in the Son, how is it that we have forgotten the splendor of our original condition and have lost our essence as bearers of the Divine Life?[36]

According to Henry, the forgetfulness in question does not arise from external conditions but is paradoxically rooted in the very process in which Life generates in itself the "Myself" such that the very condition of being a Son of God in the Son is dissimulated with the very genesis of this condition. Through the very birth of Myself, this me or this myself does not cease to forget this birth, namely, its condition of Son.[37]

Like in *L'essence*, Henry appeals to a hiddenness that, by virtue of its self-generation, reveals itself only as radical immanence; but this is a self-generation that is nevertheless the essence of the human being, *who because passively given to itself,* actively loses itself in the world and becomes forgetful of the "Myself" in the self-generation of God.

With respect to the human being's condition as Son of God in the Son, Henry describes three modes of forgetfulness: (1) the transcendental illusion of the ego, (2) the system of egoism, and (3) Care. Let me briefly describe the significance of each mode of forgetfulness.

Transcendental Illusion

Being given to itself, in an originally passive manner as this individual self, as myself, the individual is given as the power to be, in Husserl's terms, as "I can," in Heidegger's terms, as "ability-to-be." The individual awakens to itself with the ability to exercise powers, corporeal and intellectual, however limited or expansive. This is the way in which the individual takes up its passive self-givenness. Freely exercising these powers, abilities, or "ability," the self, the ego, or human being takes itself as the source of these powers, as their origin, and even more radically, as the source of its own being. The transcendental illusion of the ego arises by the ego taking itself as the foundation of its own being. So when the ego takes itself as its own condition, it forgets its true condition; it both forgets Life, which in its Ipseity gives the ego to

---

36. Henry, *C'est moi la vérité*, 166–67; Henry, *I Am the Truth*, 131–32.
37. Henry, *C'est moi la vérité*, 170; Henry, *I Am the Truth*, 135.

itself and all its powers and capacities, and it falsifies this twofold gift as the work of the ego itself. *The transcendental illusion of the ego reverses the gift of Life* that receives passively and takes it as if it were its own active accomplishment.

The System of Egoism

In describing the second mode of forgetfulness, Henry explains the cause of the so-called transcendental illusion and in so doing exhibits the truth, reality, and essential necessity of this "illusion." The gift by which Life gives itself to itself by giving the ego to itself enables the ego really to be in possession of itself and of each of its powers; it is really free in the exercise of them.[38] This is the system of egoism: Exercising the "I can"/"I am" enables me to take myself as a self-grounding ego and obfuscate the condition of the ego as Myself. The issue is that I, "Myself," persistently superimpose myself on my condition of Son, but without the latter, there would be neither "myself," nor "I," nor power of any sort.[39]

The reason that the obfuscation of the condition of the Son is not merely an illusion is that not only am I not the source of my own powers; I am also not the source of my forgetfulness of the source. This source, which is the self-givenness of absolute Life, gives the ego to itself and gives the ego the power of disposition over its own powers. Through this it dissimulates that it is not the source of its own power. But, asserts Henry, this forgetfulness would not be possible if the source itself did not constantly dissimulate itself.[40] Invisible by nature, radically immanent and never exposing itself in the "outside" of the world, this Life completely retreats in itself, allowing the ego to ignore it, precisely at that point when the ego exercises the power that Life gives it and that it attributes to itself. Thus, through the self-hiddenness of the self-generation of absolute Life, the more one takes up the gift of exercising one's ability to be, the more the ego forgets the Life, which gives the ego to itself as a myself. In this way, the forgetfulness by the human being of its condition of the Son (i.e., egoism) is not an argument against the Son, but—argues Henry—is its consequence and its proof.[41]

---

38.   Henry, *C'est moi la vérité*, 178–79; Henry, *I Am the Truth*, 141–42.
39.   Henry, *C'est moi la vérité*, 178–79; Henry, *I Am the Truth*, 141.
40.   Henry, *C'est moi la vérité*, 179; Henry, *I Am the Truth*, 142.
41.   Henry, *C'est moi la vérité*, 189; Henry, *I Am the Truth*, 150.

Care

The third mode of forgetfulness implied by the latter is what Henry calls Care. Care—an allusion to Heidegger's *Sorge*—is a style of relating to oneself, projecting oneself outside in the world. In Care, the ego attends only to itself as in the world.[42]

These three modes of forgetfulness constitute an original (ontological) forgetfulness that is rooted in Life itself as radical immanence. Life, which is alien to all apparition of itself in the world, is not separated from itself. It is not represented in thought, does not manifest itself in images, and does not conform to the structure of intentionality. Henry elaborates upon this, explaining that Life is incapable of thinking of itself, positing itself before itself, and thus, for example, remembering itself, because as we saw above, remembering has the intentional structure of thought. Hence, concludes Henry, "Life is forgetfulness, forgetfulness of itself in a radical sense." It is radical because it cannot be transformed into a correlative remembering as if it pertained to an object in the world. This forgetfulness of Life is "definitive, insurmountable" and hence "Immemorial."[43] Life escapes all possible memory because God is not transcendence; God is the radical immanence of self-affection such that it precludes a distance required for remembering.

In this case, forgetfulness concerns what has arrived before I am and not what I am without knowing it. Except for Christ, we have already forgotten our condition of Sonship, and there is never an I can without a co-eval forgetting. Forgetfulness is a forgetfulness of the enjoyment constituted by the reciprocal interiority of Father and Son, of self-affection, where there is no ego. It is the always already forgotten, the Archi-Ancience maintained in an Archi-Forgetfulness.[44]

Although we may see certain obvious parallels between *Essence* and *I Am the Truth* (such as the structure of immanence and transcendence, ontological hiddenness and self-dissimulation, forgetfulness, etc.), there is a decisive difference that concerns the process of overcoming forgetfulness. In addition to this work being replete with expressions like "rediscovering absolute Life" and "conquering Forgetfulness," Henry explicitly addresses the possibility of overcoming this primordial given Forgetfulness and of finding once more this absolute

---

42. Henry, *C'est moi la vérité*, 181, 182; Henry, *I Am the Truth*, 143, 144.
43. Henry, *C'est moi la vérité*, 186; Henry, *I Am the Truth*, 147.
44. Henry, *C'est moi la vérité*, 190–91; Henry, *I Am the Truth*, 151.

immanence that never ceases to engender its own life. If there were ever a question that overcoming forgetfulness were a matter of philosophical reflection, now it is clear that Christianity, in Henry, provides the possibility for overcoming forgetfulness, a forgetfulness that is both original and necessary. This overcoming is not an epistemological project but is a matter of salvation. Christianity affirms the possibility of the human being overcoming this radical Forgetfulness, which is to say, the possibility of rejoining the absolute Life of God. "Such a possibility signifies nothing other for it than salvation."[45]

For Henry, it is precisely within the condition of Sonship and through the mediation of Christ (not outside of this condition in the world or on the order of consciousness, knowledge, and science) that one is saved, a condition that is the Christian definition of human being; Christianity provides for human being's salvation and the ability to rediscover absolute Life in its own life in the face of original forgetfulness, the ability to live as a transcendental Myself, a Myself given to myself, to live a life that "I" do not give to myself but that is given to me in the givenness to itself of Absolute Life (i.e., God).[46] Only on the prior condition of being a Son can I both become a "lost Son" and rediscover this originary Sonship in the Son as the Son of God, identifying myself with this Divine Life.[47]

Rediscovering Sonship and surmounting Forgetfulness demands a double overcoming as it were: first, rediscovering the life of the ego as a Myself, which is to say, a Myself who is given to myself, and second, a Myself who is given to myself only in the self-givenness of absolute Life through the mediation of Christ. This is what Henry calls a "second birth" that takes place through a transmutation, a transmutation that transforms the ego into the Life of the absolute.[48]

How does this transformation come about? Is there anything "I" can do, lost as "I" am—essentially—in this forgetfulness? How can I or to what extent can I effect its recovery? Is this rediscovery already somehow effected for me or affected in me?

---

45. Henry, *C'est moi la vérité*, 190–91; Henry, *I Am the Truth*, 151; translation slightly altered.
46. Henry, *C'est moi la vérité*, 192, 193; Henry, *I Am the Truth*, 152, 153.
47. Henry, *C'est moi la vérité*, 203; Henry, *I Am the Truth*, 160–61.
48. Henry, *C'est moi la vérité*, 208–209; Henry, *I Am the Truth*, 165.

Overcoming Forgetfulness, Second Birth, and the Salvific Role of "Doing"

The overcoming of forgetfulness requires a self-transformation, and this consists, writes Henry, not in a re-cognition, but in a doing [*un faire*] that Henry initially distinguishes from acting [*agir*]—although in later chapters of this work, he will revert to the term "acting" and use it in two different ways. (For the sake of consistency, I will maintain his initial terminological distinction.) Doing, which is later called this "other acting,"[49] is an "acting" from the transcendental ego as Myself or as Son and thus a "veritable acting." Acting simpliciter as worldly action takes place from the empirical ego, from the human being as belonging to the world, as self-grounding. In this latter sense, acting does not reveal the internal possibility of acting without which acting would not be possible; as exterior comportment, it does not have the power to exhibit the reality intrinsic to it (namely, the reality of acting) because it presupposes the self-giving of Life. Doing, on the other hand, contains reality; in fact, doing realizes a real shift, for reality moves from the world to Life, and intersubjective relations move from a relation of ego to ego, to that of Son to Son.[50]

Redirecting the individual to its true essence is a doing rooted in Christian Ethics.[51] The genius of Christian Ethics, contends Henry, is that it indicates the concrete conditions within everyday life, a life which is accessible to all, by which the ego is changed into the Life of God; it indicates how the condition of the Son allows one to rediscover this condition.[52] Accordingly, rather than a re-cognition or an acting on the order of transcendence, doing might therefore be called a "re-conditioning," a re-conditioning of the ego.

Doing is accomplishing works of mercy implied in all charity, such as feeding the hungry, clothing the naked, caring for the sick, consoling the afflicted, converting sinners, or pardoning one's enemies. But just what more exactly is the difference between this "doing" peculiar to Christian Ethics (and my self-transformation into the Son of God, a re-condition on the basis of the condition of the Son—my salvation) and an acting, power, my ability to be, which stem from the ego as "I can" and "I think" and are on the order of manifestation and transcendence?

---

49. Henry, *C'est moi la vérité*, 243; Henry, *I Am the Truth*, 194.
50. Henry, *C'est moi la vérité*, 300–303, 317; Henry, *I Am the Truth*, 240–43; 254.
51. Henry, *C'est moi la vérité*, 209; Henry, *I Am the Truth*, 165–66.
52. Henry, *C'est moi la vérité*, 210; Henry, *I Am the Truth*, 166–67.

Acting consists in putting into operation a power that can be exercised only in terms of my self-possession, as if I were self-grounding; this is the condition of the "I can" that defines the ego. Acting furthermore takes absolute Life as if it were manifest in images in the world, contributing to the forgetfulness of absolute Life. Doing, however, breaks decisively with the usual representations of action, which are those of Classical and Modern thought, for doing is no longer carried out in view of the ego who acts from itself; it is no longer the power proper to the ego who says "I can." In this way, doing is different from the ensemble of powers at one's disposal. For Henry, the power of the ego is redirected to the hyper-power of absolute Life in which it is given to itself in a decisive transmutation. This decisive transformation takes place in the *work of mercy*. The ego forgets itself in such a transformation such that in and through this forgetfulness of the ego, an essential Ipseity is revealed. This Ipseity is not its own self, but what gives this self to itself in making a Self: "the self-givenness of absolute Life in the Ipseity of which this life is given to itself. It is no longer myself who acts, it is the Archi-Son who acts in me." [53]

Acting, therefore, is qualified by the ego as my power and my disposition of powers, an acting that takes its point of departure from the ego. Doing precisely as the work of mercy, on the other hand, is characterized as forgetfulness of the ego and bearing absolute Life as its presupposition; in doing, it is no longer me who acts, but God, or the Archi-Son of God, who acts in me. It is, for us, the difference between pride and humility. [54] This is undoubtedly why Henry writes that God reveals Himself in mercy. [55]

Forgetfulness, the Immemorial, is lifted not by remembering or knowledge or action of the world, but by a kind of doing that practices or more precisely eventuates in a new kind of forgetfulness, the forgetfulness of the self. In this way, accomplishing works of mercy allows the ego to overcome the forgetfulness of its condition of Son and to rediscover the Power of which it is born, accomplishing its salvation; for from works of mercy flow salvation for those who accomplish them, perdition for those who do not. [56]

---

53. Henry, *C'est moi la vérité*, 213; also, 216; Henry, *I Am the Truth*, 169; translation slightly altered; also, 171.
54. See Steinbock, *Moral Emotions*, Chapters 1 and 7.
55. Henry, *C'est moi la vérité*, 237; Henry, *I Am the Truth*, 188.
56. Henry, *C'est moi la vérité*, 210, 322; Henry, *I Am the Truth*, 166–67; 257–58.

Does this mean that we are saved through works, and does this depreciate the role of faith? To respond to this question, it is necessary to invoke an important distinction employed by Henry. The "works" that are opposed to faith are precisely "human works," works coming from a power that is putatively our own, from the self-originating human being (i.e., mundane works).[57] Accordingly, the real tension is not between faith and works, not between the "beautiful soul" and the acting of the real Politiker, not between the "Yogi and the Commissar," as Merleau-Ponty once put it, but between doing as immanent carrying out of the commandment of love, and acting as transcendent or worldly undertaking, where doing is just this condition of acting.[58]

"To do" in mercy, then, is to practice the very givenness to myself of Myself in the Archi-givenness of absolute Life and is "nothing more and nothing other than" the self-accomplishment of absolute Life.[59] It is only because doing [*faire*] is the doing of life that it can be that which makes [*fait*] life, namely, absolute self-givenness, the self-revelation of Life in which and under the form of which the revelation of God is accomplished.[60]

Acting, which is in my power, is exterior action of the world; it can be recognized objectively by others and carried out according to the objectivity of the law and validity of action. Doing, on the contrary, is in principle invisible in the sense that it is not subject to the laws of manifestation; having nothing "to do" with the manifestation of the world, it reveals the Truth of Life, which is interior, inaccessible to external observation, subject neither to objectivity nor to the letter of the law.[61] Doing designates this interior, "passive" self-transformation of life; for Henry, it finds here its unique motivation and purpose as well as the very milieu where it is accomplished and where it is possible.[62] Doing, then, is not my doing because Christ who brings Life to human beings, brings human beings to Life.[63] The mediation of Christ functions as a call from Christ to follow Him who gives me True life. This call is not the law, but the commandment to love my neighbor as myself; one can love the Divine Life in oneself and at the same time

---

57. Henry, *C'est moi la vérité*, 242–43; Henry, *I Am the Truth*, 193.
58. Henry, *C'est moi la vérité*, 295, 299–300; Henry, *I Am the Truth*, 236–37; 239–40.
59. Henry, *C'est moi la vérité*, 212–15; Henry, *I Am the Truth*, 168–70.
60. Henry, *C'est moi la vérité*, 216; Henry, *I Am the Truth*, 171.
61. Henry, *C'est moi la vérité*, 219–23; Henry, *I Am the Truth*, 173–77.
62. Henry, *C'est moi la vérité*, 218; Henry, *I Am the Truth*, 173.
63. Henry, *C'est moi la vérité*, 161; Henry, *I Am the Truth*, 127–28.

love one's neighbor as oneself because the Other is also the Son of God, like me-Myself. Doing is revealed as the essence of acting, for the latter's pretension of containing reality objectively is challenged and shown up as only an appearance, and a fallacious one at that.[64]

Thus, we find that Christian ethics makes a distinction that rejoins or conforms with others made so far "phenomenologically" concerning immanence and transcendence, and revelation and manifestation. On the one hand, doing is an accomplishment of "invisible Life," interior to Life itself; on the other hand, action is manifest in the world, taking its departure from the self, oriented toward the world, and in this sense external to the condition of the Son. The former is revelatory of my essence, "Myself," the Son of God in the Son; the latter is mere appearance, irreal, a product of transcendental illusion. Doing is the practice of mercy as the forgetfulness of self; acting is the reinforcement of the ego as the forgetfulness of the condition of Sonship. Doing is the essence of acting just as immanence is the essence of transcendence and revelation the essence of manifestation. Through doing, one forgets oneself, loses one's self as mundane human being and through this forgetfulness gains myself as the Son of God in the Son. Doing, therefore, is an accomplishment that results in salvation, acting on the contrary leads to perdition.

4. FORGETFULNESS OR IDOLATRY? DOING-ACTS OF MERCY AND THE GLORY OF GOD

In my final section of this chapter, I assess the appropriateness of speaking of forgetfulness within the phenomenological reflections of Henry. I both contrast it with a concept that is more suited to the religious and moral context of Henry's undertaking and modestly pose some questions concerning several implications that forgetfulness has in such a context. My final section will be ordered in the following way along the lines of these concerns: doing-acts of mercy, individuation and exemplarity, the language of forgetfulness and hiddenness, and idolatry as reversal.

---

64. Henry, *C'est moi la vérité*, 222, 301; Henry, *I Am the Truth*, 175–76; 241.

The Efficacy of Doing-Acts

"To do" acts of mercy is to practice the very givenness of myself to Myself in the Archi-givenness of absolute Life. To do acts of mercy is to practice Christian ethics according to Henry, which following the commandment of love, is to love one's neighbor as oneself, in humility and poverty (e.g., to clothe the naked, feed the hungry, forgive my enemies *qua* Sons of God in the Son). In this way I do not treat the other person as a creature who is differentiated in space and time as an ego, but as a transcendental Myself, as absolutely singular, generated in the self-generation of God, like I Myself am a Son of God in the Son.

Distinguishing doing from acting (even if in an implicit manner) does make good sense in some respects. One can always put on the exterior countenance of fasting—one can literally act as if one were fasting but not really hold to the spirit of fasting; likewise, one can act in the world in a way that is not taking the commandment of love seriously.[65] Moreover, one could exteriorly feed the hungry and effect an external change all the while having many different motivations in mind: I may want to feel good about myself, I may want to put "community work" on a curriculum vitae, and so on. Or conversely, I may want to effect a change in the world out of the commandment of love, but try as I might, all my actions may be ineffectual and to this extent in vain. Should one's salvation depend upon actually effecting such an external change in the world? Is there a limit to when that change is effected? Now? Generations in the future? It is true that one can pretend to be loving toward another and really be preparing acts of violence; but can one love one's neighbor as one's Self, as a Son of God, and still do-acts of violence? Can one, for example, enslave others (being well meaning or not) and further the Kingdom of God?

For Henry, then, the point of practicing mercy is not to conform to an exterior model and to imitate the show of mercy, but to live in such a way that the acts, whatever they may be, bear the essence of mercy. To borrow a distinction that Scheler makes, one does not live "like" Christ in the sense of copying the exterior operations (having long hair, being a carpenter's son, etc.), but living "as" Christ such that whatever the acts may be (though they cannot be just anything), they bear inextricably the essence of or internal sense of that life, though they are

---

65. Henry, *C'est moi la vérité*, 244–52; Henry, *I Am the Truth*, 194–201.

irreducible to that essence.[66] So if the commandment to love one's neighbor as a Son of God in the Son is to make any concrete sense, would not practicing mercy not only be a recondition of the self, but also effect change in the world, in a decisive way? And if not, does Christianity prescribe a fleeing from the world?

Such questions and objections are anticipated by Henry.[67] To grasp the full import of Henry's response and to see whether some aspect of these objections remains, it is important to understand just what Henry means by "world." This is where the issues raised thus far become delicate, demanding a clarification of the relation between doing and acting.

By "world," Henry tends to understand two things. First, for the most part, world is taken to be what is objectivistic, what falls under the rubric of objective reality, what is empirically determined and subject to causal laws, or again a natural reality that is inherently mathematizable. (This would correspond in Husserl to the scientific worldview that defines human being or the "naturalistic" attitude.) It should also be noted here that by world we understand not just what falls on the side of the "object," but on the side of the "subject" as well. For I can take myself and others for granted and/or subject them, for example, to the economy of exchange value.[68] But this is not and cannot be the only definition of world, even though the term is often used in this way by Henry. "World" is also employed as what we live every day and what we get when we take its source for granted. (This corresponds, in part, to the commonsense worldview that defines human being and the more general sense of the "natural" attitude in Husserl.) Of course, by taking the source of the world for granted, we can easily slip into an objective, quantitative view of reality (the naturalistic attitude), and in this way, the former is founded in the latter. But by itself, the everyday concept

66. See Max Scheler, *Die Formalismus in der Ethik und die materiale Wertethik*, ed. Maria Scheler (München: Francke Verlag, 1966), 563 ff. See Anthony J. Steinbock, "Interpersonal Attention through Exemplarity," *Journal of Consciousness Studies: Beyond Ourselves*, ed. Evan Thompson (2001), 179–96.

67. Henry, *C'est moi la vérité*, 292–323; Henry, *I Am the Truth*, 234–58.

68. Henry, *C'est moi la vérité*, 304 ff.; Henry, *I Am the Truth*, 243 ff.

of the world is irreducible to the former and rejoins another fundamental notion also used by Henry, namely, transcendence.[69]

Having clarified these two concepts of world, it makes sense to say, following Henry, that the Transcendental Myself or the Christian (which for Henry is the same thing) is not mundane or worldly because she or he does not take the source of the world for granted, does not live from the world, but rather lives from the source of the world. Further, if we limit the concept of world to the first sense, Christianity would not require a transformation of the world in the sense of bringing into the world an objective, quantitatively assessable, empirical modification in accordance with its laws, utilizing them, producing, thanks to them, a change that is always presented under the form of an objective determination.[70]

But if we take world or mundaneity as the everyday world of life whose source is taken for granted—a sense that rejoins the early meaning of transcendence—then transcendental phenomenology (or Christianity) is the clarification of the "internal" meaning of world, illuminating its "source" so as not to live in forgetfulness; if, in this sense, it is a clarification of the world that we live in and not that we live from, then the world cannot be separate from the source, or in different terms, transcendence cannot be separate from immanence, because it is qualified now by immanence as an immanent transcendence, and Christianity (and the doing peculiar to it) would have to be a transformation of the world, not according to the laws of the world (objective reality, quantification, even commonsense forgetfulness), but from the "source." This would mean a transformation of the transcendental Myself, a change in style.

Henry is himself quick to point out that doing (immanent doing) is not non-acting because doing works of mercy is precisely acting: The Good Samaritan is acting when he leans over the person covered with blood to assist him and care for him. And who, he asks, constructed the first hospitals in the Middle Ages?[71] Here, I understand Henry to be

---

69. Again, these two ways in which Henry speaks of world correspond to two ways in which Husserl explains the natural attitude and being "mundane"—two ways that are also sometimes conflated by Husserl—the naturalistic and the natural attitude. Although the naturalistic worldview is a possibility within the natural, the reverse is not necessarily the case. For one can take the source of the world for granted in the sense of living immediately in the everyday lifeworld, and one can reduce the world to quantified being within the scientific view of the world.

70. Henry, *C'est moi la vérité*, 295; Henry, *I Am the Truth*, 236.

71. Henry, *C'est moi la vérité*, 298; Henry, *I Am the Truth*, 238–39.

suggesting that the doing, which is an acting, is not objective action, not action undertaken according to mundane laws or according to the truth of the world. But Henry seems to fall short of explicitly asserting that this is a *transformation of the world*. Certainly, the problem is not as patent as it is in Heidegger, but it does at least raise the specter of Heidegger's "esotericism" of Being without beings (see Chapter 2).

This is where I see the difficulty if I understand Henry correctly. On the one hand, we have a living from the source, an immanent acting or doing, on the other, the truth of the world, where living in the world seems to be limited to living from the world.

But is not, for example, doing works of mercy the transformation of the world, not from the world, but from the source of the world in the world? When Henry writes of the "paradoxes of Christianity," are not these paradoxes caused by, at least in part, "intertwinings" of immanence and transcendence, *intertwinings* that do not allow such a separation of immanence and transcendence?[72] *I am given to myself as a gift in the world of life, given the power to live.* It is already a relation of immanence and transcendence with others, the integration of the religious and the moral. Is there any evidence that the gift in the world of life would be retracted?[73]

Henry writes that this is the paradoxical condition of the ego: On the one hand, it is completely itself, having in some respect its own "phenomenological substance," that is, its own life such as it experiences it. On the other hand, it is nothing by itself; its own phenomenological substance is the self-affection from a phenomenological substance absolutely different from it, from a power other than his own, a power of which it is absolutely devoid. This is the power of absolute Life casting itself into life and of living. The former is absolute, the latter is relative.[74]

Is this not also the same paradox peculiar to the body? Again, when describing the body, Henry appeals to the same separation peculiar to immanence and transcendence cited above: the body seeing and the body seen, or more drastically, the body in the Truth of Life, the invisible body, the living body, and the body-object, an object like other

---

72. I write this realizing that for Henry, given the way he has described the phenomenological structure of immanence and transcendence, it is absurd for immanence and transcendence to intertwine.

73. See Anthony J. Steinbock, *Limit-Phenomena and Phenomenology in Husserl* (London: Rowman & Littlefield, 2017), esp. Chapter 2.

74. Henry, *C'est moi la vérité*, 263; Henry, *I Am the Truth*, 210.

bodies in the universe, the body as *res extensa*. Does this characterization adequately reflect the phenomenon of the body, of incarnation/Incarnation? It would seem that a transcendental phenomenology of the body, which clarifies the body from its source, could not maintain the separation just mentioned, for at a very minimum the so-called "body-object" could no longer be determined as *res extensa*, but would demand a different characterization of it. Just because the body is not essentially *res extensa*, does not mean that the only phenomenological aspect of the body is the Invisible body. Would not treating the body from its source through a transcendental clarification of incarnation imply the intertwining of immanence and transcendence?[75]

I suggest that rather than there being a problem with Henry's analyses, there is a tension between his analyses and some of his assertions. With this in mind, I think we would have to say that doing does qualify (i.e., transform) the world itself, not from the world but from the source of the world in the world; in this sense, doing redeems the world as world; it is possible for the world, institutions, the body, and so on to bear the meaning of "good" or "holy." And this means that practicing mercy would not simply issue in my salvation, but would issue in historical and direct challenges to various forms of violence: to battering, to the commodification and reifications of other persons, to ecological exploitation, and so on, all of which are founded in what we will come to understand as "idolatry." Doing-acts of mercy is a critique of historical forms and "worldly" institutions of violence, a critique of idolatry. But then doing-acts of mercy would have to amount to the direct participation with the other as loving (see Chapter 5). Doing-acts is not a critique of historical, worldly forms because they are worldly,

---

75. Even though Henry has addressed the issue of incarnation as an archaeology of the flesh—incarnation understood both in a general sense and in a Christian sense—it does not fundamentally alter the basic set of problems addressed here. See Michel Henry, *Incarnation: une philosophie de la chair* (Paris: Seuil, 2000). Michel Henry, *Incarnation: A Philosophy of Flesh*, trans. Karl Hefty (Evanston, IL: Northwestern University Press, 2015). I cannot elaborate upon this idea here, but it goes to Michel Henry's great credit to be able to read profoundly different authors and subjects in such a strikingly consistent way. He is able to see and describe the same movement of the "essence of manifestation" in the context of religious thought, in Husserl, in psychoanalysis, and in political thought. His nearly 1,000-page monumental work on Marx [Michel Henry, *Marx* (Paris: Gallimard, 1976)]—comparable in size to his *Essence*—is testimony to this feat. He is able to describe in Marx's thought—from his young humanist tendencies, through the *Grundrisse*, to his "mature" works on capital—the same dynamic of immanence and transcendence described in all of his works. For me, however, this still issues in the same set of questions regarding the problem of forgetfulness and the ultimate significance of individuation and transcendence.

but because they do not bear the meaning of mercy or the commandment of love (i.e., they can be challenged qua evil).

Because practicing mercy demands that the acts bear the essence of
mercy in whatever exterior form those acts take, and because a phenomenology of mercy would show, ultimately, that it is not possible to
separate the immanence of doing from the transcendence of acting, I
find it appropriate to express this phenomenon by hyphenating it in this
way: "doing-acts." For practicing mercy as *doing-acts* of mercy does
mean concretely, though inexhaustibly, sheltering the homeless, giving
instruction to those who are ignorant, which does effect a change in the
world. This change, moreover, would have to be seen as an essential
transformation, a transformation that qualifies our relation to the essence, effecting the "Kingdom of God on earth (where this effect is not
just an incidental result of doing mercy). It is through doing-acts that
one intervenes in the world and thereby transforms the essence of the
world, the essence of manifestation, Divine Life. This transformation,
however, can go in the direction of either good or evil, for it is possible
in the face of the revelation of absolute Life not to do-acts of mercy, to
do-acts of evil, and this places a profound responsibility on us when we
do-acts of any sort. It is a responsibility suggested by a relation that
Scheler has called a solidarity of love not only between finite persons,
but between finite persons and infinite Person.[76]

This leads to a set of related questions concerning individuation,
absolute self-affection, and a problematic relative self-affection.

Absolute Self-Affection and Transcendental Life

For Henry, the individual is not differentiated by virtue of being a
creature of the world endowed with reason or by virtue of spatio-
temporal location; the body is not the principle of individuation; rather,
one is absolutely singular as a transcendental Myself by being given to
myself as irreducibly different in one and the same Life, and through
Christian ethics, loving one's neighbor as oneself, as the Son of God in
the Son, like me.[77] Each one is distinctive and not lost in anonymity
because I am given to myself as Myself, as unique and irreplaceable by
receiving the commandment to love my neighbor as Myself I receive
Myself, passively, in the accusative, as singularly Myself. According to

76. See Max Scheler, *Die Idee des Friedens und der Pazifismus* (Berlin: Der Neue
Geist, 1931), fn. 20 ff.
77. Henry, *C'est moi la vérité*, 164–65; Henry, *I Am the Truth*, 130–31.

Henry, to be an individual is to be a living transcendental Myself such that the concept of the individual and the concept of Life are joined from the very start.[78] The question bears on how they are joined. Although this passivity, this passively received individuation, is original, it cannot be exhaustive, for precisely as origin, it is origin-originating. This is to say that the origin is taken up in such a way that the origin continues "to accomplish" the individuation of the individual as singularly unique, or in Scheler's terms, as "absolute." On this point I disagree with Henry that the distinction to be made is that between the self-affection of absolute Life in which this life is self-engendered, and the relative self-affection, in which the ego experiences itself as given to itself, but not by itself.[79] The distinction cannot be *between an absolute and a relative self-affection, but between an absolute self-affection that is infinite, and an absolute self-affection that is finite*, an intertwining of infinite and finite. Otherwise, we land back in the esotericism of Heidegger, and of the gift being merely retained in the Giving, but not Giving's presence in the gift. Being not self-grounding, receiving Myself, does not mean the dissolution of Myself in the infinite.

Because Henry views the former as absolute and the latter as relative, he can write that in the final analysis there is only *one self-affection, "that of absolute Life."* This is because the self-affection in which the ego is given to itself is *only* the self-affection of *absolute Life that gives it, the ego, to itself in the process of giving itself to itself*.[80] This is one of the "paradoxes of Christianity" to which I alluded above. But if we are to take this "paradox" seriously, we have to ask just how seriously we are to take the "gift" of ourselves to ourselves, the gift of being an "ego," of living in the world—even when not from the world, as has been pointed out, but from the source in the world. Is not the gift made "absolute," though finite? Is there any evidence that it is retracted?[81] Is not taking up the gift of ourselves to ourselves absolute, though as finite?

On this view, individuation takes place through doing-acts that appropriate the commandment positively or negatively, qualifying the person precisely as this person like no other, constituting, as it were, a style of Sonship that is decisive in the sense of irreplaceably distinctive

---

78. Henry, *C'est moi la vérité*, 150; Henry, *I Am the Truth*, 119.
79. Henry, *C'est moi la vérité*, 263; Henry, *I Am the Truth*, 210.
80. Henry, *C'est moi la vérité*, 263; Henry, *I Am the Truth*, 210.
81. See Steinbock, *Limit-Phenomena and Phenomenology in Husserl*, Chapter 2.

or personal: absolute, unique. This is the generation of my self-generation in the self-generation of absolute Life.

But for this to be the case, one could not say that our doing-acts,
especially, doing-acts of mercy are *"nothing more and nothing other
than"* the self-accomplishment of absolute Life.[82] This is not to say that
God is not the sustaining Power, that I am not originally given to
myself as Myself, that doing-acts of mercy is not *also* the accomplishment of absolute Life; it is not an attempt to hold on desperately to the
ego in pride (for we can still distinguish the person as absolutely unique
from the system of egoism).[83] Rather, it is to suggest that we are qualified in this doing-acts, where this doing-acts is creative and originating, and that if one is stripped of this, if it is absolutely "no longer Myself doing acts of mercy," then loving my neighbor as My-self can have
no moral tenor.

It is also to suggest that by doing these and those acts, this *unique*
person is the presence of God, that it is also possible in the presence of
God not to do-acts of mercy, possible to take up the "commandment" in
a negative way, bringing evil into the world; it is possible not to hasten
the "Kingdom of God"; it is to say that if someone like "Mother Teresa" can do-acts of mercy, the fact that she (absolute, unique, finite
person) can do this is the glory of God. Finally, it is to try to make
sense precisely of "creation" (for if transcendence is radically foreign
to God in Henry, it is not clear just what the point of the world is); it is
to assert that transcendence in all its forms is not superfluous.

The significance of the commandment of loving in Christianity, or
tzedakah in Judaism, would disappear if it were only and exhaustively
God acting in me (which is not to say that I as Myself, do not act from
God). If doing-acts of mercy were nothing more and nothing other than
God acting in me, where would we find the "glory of God"?

Furthermore, can the "sole motivation" for doing-acts of mercy be
the self-transformation of life?[84] Or is there not another motivation
rooted in the uniqueness or "absolute singularity" of the other person as
well? For whom do I do-acts of mercy or against whom do I do-acts of
evil?

Finally, I think that we have to interpret doing-acts as a continuation
of the self-generation of the absolute in a unique mode, which is this
person. The individuation of the person as this person that is accom-

---

82. Henry, *C'est moi la vérité*, 212–15; Henry, *I Am the Truth*, 168–70.
83. See Steinbock, *Moral Emotions*, Chapters 1 and 7.
84. Henry, *C'est moi la vérité*, 218; Henry, *I Am the Truth*, 172–73.

plished through doing-acts would be understood as the revelation of God in me-Myself. By being revealed as unique in doing-acts as uniquely me-Myself, God is revealed in me-Myself, which is simultaneously a pointing back to absolute Life. The individual finite life becomes exemplary of absolute infinite Life and bears the structure of revealing-revealed; God is clarified (or obfuscated) accordingly. In this way, Christ, who for Henry is the commandment to love, is exemplary as a pointer back to the self-generation of absolute Life. And with a different nuance, so too is the individual person.

Hiddenness and Forgetfulness

It is my task in other works to distinguish between various modes of givenness: epiphany, revelation, manifestation, exposure, display, and disclosure, to describe their interconnections, and to show how "person" and "life" are given uniquely in each of them, religiously, morally, and aesthetically.[85] Henry would agree that God is not "given" the way an object is manifest in transcendence because the Essence of absolute Life has a unique mode of givenness proper to its essence, namely, revelation. To this extent it might make sense to say that immanence is hidden from the manifestation of the world as the world is given to transcendence. To think otherwise would be to fall prey to ontological monism or the forgetfulness of the condition of Sonship.

But it seems to me mistaken to say that immanence is not given to transcendence, for of course immanence is given to transcendence in many ways (as person, for example). But for Henry, this givenness is precisely taking place in a passive, impotent manner (not being at our disposal) in the mode of revelation. Because there is another mode of givenness that does not conform to the manifestation of the world—revelation—it further seems gratuitous to speak as if immanence would *withdraw* itself unilaterally.

Is it possible to speak of hiddenness, withdrawal, dissimulation, where revelation is concerned? Again, we confront the problem encountered above with Heidegger. If God cannot be given except through self-revelation in loving, then as Scheler remarks, no absolutely good personal God "could" refrain from revelation.[86] Withdrawing,

---

85. See Steinbock, *Phenomenology and Mysticism*, and Steinbock, *Moral Emotions*. See also Anthony J. Steinbock, *Beloved, Loving, and Hating in the Schema of the Heart*, in preparation.

86. Scheler, *Vom Ewigen im Menschen*, 333, 342.

concealing/disclosing would belong only to the ontology of manifestation. In short, the "source" cannot "constantly dissimulate itself," at
least in terms of self-revelation.[87] What, then, is the motivation for
"forgetfulness"?[88]

For Henry, this self-dissimulation of the source is the foundation for
the forgetfulness of the source. Being firmly rooted in the phenomenological tradition, as is Henry, it certainly makes sense to employ the
term "forgetfulness" to evoke an omission as radical and as pervasive
as the obfuscation of revelation in favor of a myopic emphasis on
manifestation, which amounts to saying, the reduction of revelation to
manifestation. But if this is to mean something more than a philosophical mishap or even a (fundamental) distortion in our relation with God,
the term forgetfulness is perhaps misleading, at best.[89]

Strictly speaking, if there is removal from the "source," from absolute Life, from infinite absolute Person, is it because of the Source? Is
forgetfulness a thrown forgetfulness, as "gift" of some sort? In brief,
using the conceptual framework of hiddenness and forgetfulness oper-
ates with a conflation and is not insignificant: a conflation of the withdrawal of Being with the absolute infinite Person as self-revealing in

---

87. Henry, *C'est moi la vérité*, 179; Henry, *I Am the Truth*, 141–42.
88. See Steinbock, *Phenomenology and Mysticism*.
89. In the first case, if immanence "essentially" recuses itself from manifestation,
allowing transcendence to be given to itself, not only can immanence not be remem-
bered within the intentionality of consciousness, as origin-originating; it cannot be forgotten, either. This does not mean, of course, that immanence is not given in some other
way, and this is precisely Henry's point, namely, that (1) immanence is revealed in a
revelation that is not subject to remembering, and (2) the reason we tend to omit the
possibility of revelation as a mode of givenness is due to "ontological monism," the
historical restriction of givenness to one type of givenness, manifestation. Accordingly,
transcendence does not really "forget" immanence; it can occlude it, it can become
preoccupied with itself, but it cannot forget immanence as such. In fact, the terminology
of forgetfulness does more homage to Heidegger and to Husserl than it does justice to
Henry's own thought. Just how original can forgetfulness be? Is it possible to trace
forgetfulness back prior to the advent of transcendence and then to say that forgetfulness
is "original"? Does not making forgetfulness original take the perspective of transcendence toward immanence? This, however, is something of which Henry is consistently
critical; for from the very outset, Henry refuses both to address Immanence from the
perspective of transcendence and to treat our existential situation from the perspective of
secular human being. For him the very utterance of transcendence is accomplished from
Immanence.

loving, of ontology with religious experiencing, of being with person, and of forgetfulness with idolatry.[90]

CONCLUSION

It would be reductive and simplistic to maintain that Henry is only repeating Heidegger's problems only in explicitly religious (or explicitly Christian) terminology. In fact, if we were to look to a phenomenological predecessor to unlock philosophical motivations for his work, the much more evident figure would be Husserl. One could even maintain that what Lévinas does with Husserl by radicalizing the phenomenon of transcendence, Henry does with Husserl by radicalizing the phenomenon of immanence. And like Lévinas, Henry makes a distinction between different modes of givenness: for Lévinas it is between the disclosure of the object and the revelation of the "Other"; for Henry it is the manifestation of the world (or transcendence) and the revelation of Absolute Life. For Henry, the reduction of givenness to the one mode of givenness (essentially, revelation to manifestation) results in what he calls "ontological monism." This is a forgetfulness of the Essence, of Absolute Life in its Self-Affection.

The coincidence of Henry's exposition with that of Heidegger's for me concerns the leading clue of forgetfulness, which is ultimately intrinsic to the radical separation between immanence and transcendence, suggesting that Self-Affecting Absolute Life necessarily withdraws from transcendence, from the world, in a kind of fundamental forgetfulness reminiscent *mutatis mutandis* of Heidegger's "withdrawal" of the It that gives. Despite Henry's gestures toward "doing" and mercy, there is still the problem of the constitutive role of transcendence, or our acting with others, of loving or of hating. If our actions are *"nothing more and nothing other than"* the self-accomplishment of absolute Life, but a revelation that remains essentially hidden from manifestation, is this substantially different from "It" giving and essentially withdrawing yet ultimately only retaining what is given, withdrawing from "in favor of the gift," but not abandoning "It"self to or in the world,

---

90. See Steinbock, *Phenomenology and Mysticism*, Chapter 8. Although Henry does have another term available to him for forgetfulness, namely, "barbarism," it does not capture the religious and moral dimension of the problem in the same way that "idolatry" does. And see Michel Henry, *La barbarie* (Paris: Grasset, 1987). See also James Hart, "A Phenomenological Theory and Critique of Culture: A Reading of Michel Henry's *La barbarie*," *Continental Philosophy Review* 32, no. 3 (1999): 255–70.

with the "gifts"? Are all "gifts" always already retained, or in different terms, saved by virtue of immanent doing reducible to Absolute Life? Is machination, forgetfulness, evil reducible to "eventing" or nothing more and nothing other than the self-affection of Absolute Life? Do both of these articulations not lend themselves in their own ways to esotericism rather than religious experience—religious experience, which is inherently and essentially intertwined with although experientially distinct from the moral, historical, and ecological dimensions of being?

In Chapter 4, I take up a different formulation of the problem of givenness in the work of Jean-Luc Marion. I take the issue around the problem of what he characterizes as the "poor phenomenon." This treatment of Marion will also be important because it will relate to the problem of the gift and giving when I take up his articulation of the matter in the context of Maimonides.[91]

---

91. A different version of this chapter appeared in article form in a special collection on Michel Henry as "The Problem of Forgetfulness in Michel Henry," *Continental Philosophy Review* 32 (1999): 271–302.

Chapter 4

The Poor Phenomenon

Marion, Givenness, and Saturation

Today, one can hardly speak of a phenomenology of givenness without coming across or coming to terms with Jean-Luc Marion's novel conception of the "saturated phenomenon." The most radical determination of the phenomenon is not "being" or "to be," but *givenness*. The saturated phenomenon is that which subverts, overflows, exceeds, and precedes the intentional sense-giving on the part of the subject; for Marion, it is the given par excellence.

According to Marion, there are four main modes of saturated givenness, what he calls the event, the idol, the flesh, the icon, and encompassing all of them, "revelation."[1] Although the status of the saturated phenomena is relatively clear in Marion's work, and it has been the topic of many investigations, what remains ambiguous, in my view, is the phenomenal character and phenomenological status of what he calls the "poor phenomenon"—and thereby how saturation functions in relation to the so-called "mundane."

The significance of the poor phenomenon is not simply an interesting point because it concerns the thought of Marion and the exegesis of his work. It is significant philosophically because it bears on the way in

---

1. Jean Luc Marion, *Étant donné: essai d'une phenomenologie de la donation* (Paris: PUF, 1997), 314–29; hereafter, *Étant donné*. English translation by Jeffrey L. Kosky as *Being Given: Toward a Phenomenology of Givenness* (Stanford, CA: Stanford University Press, 2002), 225–37; hereafter, *Being Given*.

which we understand experiences of everyday life that fall outside of, or ostensibly fall outside of, religious, moral, and aesthetic life. Is the poverty of poor phenomena intrinsic to the things themselves? Are poor phenomena given uniformly? Is there a shortfall or corruption in givenness because of us, due to our inattention, or to our inability to receive saturated phenomena? Are there degrees of poverty like there are of saturation? Are poor phenomena essential or contingent features of our existence? Are the poor (phenomena) always with us?

In the final analysis, I am critical of Marion's characterization of saturation and poverty, not because it is uncalled for, but because he misses the implications of his own work and does not, as he should, determine poor phenomena on the basis of saturated phenomena. But even here, I suggest, the concept of the saturated phenomenon would have to give way to verticality and the process of de-limitation, founded in loving.

1. SATURATED GIVENNESS AS REVELATION

According to Marion, different kinds of phenomena can be categorized according to the different ways in which they show themselves. Something *shows* itself only insofar as it *gives* itself such that the showing can vary according to degrees of givenness.[2] Marion's work on *phenom*enology therefore centers and must center on the problem of givenness.

Because the paradigm of givenness for Marion is the saturated phenomenon (because it marks the givenness from which it comes), allow me to approach the significance of poor phenomena through the meaning of saturated givenness. This is, in fact, Marion's approach: "My entire project . . . aims to think the common-law phenomenon, and through it *the poor phenomenon*, on the basis of the paradigm of the saturated phenomenon."[3] More than the complete fulfillment of an intention, saturation is marked by an excess of intuition (i.e., givenness) over the subjective intention of meaning-giving.

There are, in the main, four ways saturation takes place, and these correspond to four types of the saturated phenomenon.[4] Saturating the

---

2. Cf. Marion, *Étant donné*, 309–10; Marion, *Being Given*, 221–22.
3. Marion, *Étant donné*, 316; Marion, *Being Given*, 227 (my emphasis).
4. See also the careful and philosophically sensitive study of Marion and modes of givenness in Christina M. Gschwandtner, *Degrees of Givenness: On Saturation in Jean-Luc Marion* (Bloomington, IN: Indiana University Press, 2014).

category of quantity is the "event." It is marked by its non-anticipatable character, its singularity, and by the fact that it is historically nonrepeatable. Evident under the aspect of the "unbearable" and "intolerable" character of the phenomenon is the "idol"; it forces us to accommodate our gaze to it, and in this sense bedazzles the perceiver, overflowing his or her ability to master it. Further, the absoluteness of the saturated phenomenon absolves itself as "flesh" from the category of relation; in its radical immediacy of auto-affection, it remains irreplaceably "mine." Finally, free from any reference to the ego, the "icon" or "face" saturates the categories of modality. The saturated phenomenon as icon is irreducible and irregardable in the sense that the face (of the Other) gives nothing to see, but in giving the *invisible* through the visible, nevertheless weighs upon "me" and is that from which I receive "myself."[5]

What is the meaning of the event, the idol, the flesh, and the icon as modes of saturation? For the purposes of this explication, and to be able to press on to the problem of the poor phenomenon, let me stay with Marion's presentation. For Marion, it is the "phenomenon of revelation" that concentrates the four types of saturated phenomena. Not merely being one among the others, revelation as the maximum of saturated phenomenality is the *essential possibility* of saturation and thus its phenomenal meaning.[6] For Marion, the privileged manifestation of the icon is Christ, and hence Christ is the example par excellence of revelation. But because, according to his own claim, Marion proceeds as a philosopher and especially as a phenomenologist, he brackets the reality of the world to liberate the phenomena and givenness (and kinds of givenness); this allows him to determine the meaning of saturation in terms of its essential possibility—revelation—without passing judgment on its existential claims. As the essential meaning of saturation, revelation is qualified by the "call," which bears the traits of the summons, surprise, interlocution, and facticity. The call, the undeniable par excellence, "in fact characterizes every saturated phenomenon as such."[7]

The effect of the saturated phenomenon on the subject, which in its most radical form is the revelatory call, not only transforms the otherwise passive object into activity and more precisely the gift; it transforms what we formerly understood in phenomenology as the giver of

---

5. See Marion, *Étant donné*, 318–25; Marion, *Being Given*, 228–33.
6. Marion, *Étant donné*, 326–28; Marion, *Being Given*, 235–36.
7. Marion, *Étant donné*, 367–71, 390–91; Marion, *Being Given*, 267, 283.

sense into the receiver, and further, the receiver radicalized now as "the gifted," the one who receives one's self from what gives itself.[8]

To sum up, the saturated phenomenon is the paradigm of givenness, whereby revelation becomes exemplary or the meaning of saturation. The essence of givenness is revelation received as the call whose transformative effect constitutes me now as the gifted one. I come back to the question of the gifted below. For now, having all too briefly determined the meaning of the saturated phenomenon as revelation, I am in a position to examine the status of the poor phenomenon.

2. THE POOR AND THE COMMON

Given that the saturated phenomenon is the paradigm of phenomena, and revelation is the paradigm of givenness, we might question the status of anything that is not a saturated phenomenon. For example, is everything else ultimately reducible to the saturated phenomenon? Is all givenness really just revelation, only at a remove? Are other phenomena derivative modes? Before determining the meaning of the poor phenomenon from a more critical perspective in the context of this work, let me remain with Marion's explication of the topic.

According to Marion, there are other types of phenomena in addition to the saturated ones. They are called the poor phenomenon and the common phenomenon. Far from being reducible to one another, he regards them all (the saturated, the poor, and the common) as "*original figures of phenomenality*," which is to say, essentially distinct, irreducible types.[9] I describe the latter two briefly and then address them in a more critical fashion.

Poor Phenomena

The poor phenomenon is initially defined as a phenomenon that is poor in intuition. To give itself, such a phenomenon does not need much more than its concept alone or its bare intelligibility; it need only admit an intuition that is formal. Because the poor phenomenon is merely formal, universal without content or material differentiation, it no longer need admit an experience that is uncertain. It is "*undurchstreichbar*,"

---

8. Marion, *Étant donné*, 366; Marion, *Being Given*, 266. And Marion, *Étant donné*, 371; Marion, *Being Given*, 269. "I receive *my self* from the call that gives me to myself before giving me anything whatsoever."

9. Marion, *Étant donné*, 310; Marion, *Being Given*, 222, my emphasis.

as Husserl might say, not able to be crossed out through subsequent experiences. Such an abstraction from content and its unproblematic iterability make it a perfect object for speculative metaphysics, and in fact, this object-ness, this objectivity, becomes for Marion the privileged form of intuition and phenomenon proper to it. "They claim only a formal intuition in mathematics or a categorial intuition in logic, in other words, a 'vision of essences' and idealities."[10]

The poor phenomenon cannot become the paradigm of givenness, therefore, because the abstract epistemological certainty of the poor phenomenon does not allow there to be an "accomplished phenomenality" (i.e., real or individual intuition or temporalization).

Common Phenomena

Common (or common-law) phenomena are initially described as different in kind from poor phenomena. Here, we are not concerned with eidetic entities that lack material individualization, but with everyday phenomena that might in principle be adequately given, but which most often are given in an inadequate manner. In short, common phenomena are those that receive fulfillment (or are disappointed) according to how they are intended. In this case, a "maximum" of givenness could only be an intuition that perfectly measures up to how I intended it.

For Marion, the model of givenness is what we might call loosely, the pragmatic object. This covers not only the phenomenon encountered in the everyday context of use, but the object that can be predicted in use because of its weak intuition, "attaining a degree of certainty comparable to that of the poor phenomena."[11] Because of the deficit of intuition, it is susceptible to my mastery. Thus, I can have a concept of what is supposed to happen or of what is supposed to appear before it actually does happen or does appear. In this way, if I cannot prevent the object disrupting my mastery over it, I can at least reduce the effect of things not going "my" way. Through my foresight, or the preeminence of the concept over intuition, I can anticipate the object in advance as already given and thus "delay" its givenness because the concept of it precedes its givenness. The technique employed where common phenomena are concerned permit and demand the repetition of the phenomena because the latter cannot tolerate an innovation or modification

---

10. Marion, *Étant donné*, 310; Marion, *Being Given*, 222, translation modified.
11. Marion, *Étant donné*, 311–12; Marion, *Being Given*, 223.

that is not governed in advance; it permits nothing surprising, novel, or unanticipated. [12]

In one respect, nothing could be clearer in Marion than these three types of phenomena: the saturated, the poor, and the common. Indeed, we already had a preview of them in his *Reduction and Givenness*. In that work, Marion wanted to open up the problem of givenness to phenomena that do not give themselves as objects or beings. Marion described the kind of objectivity that was peculiar to the "first reduction," which he called the transcendental reduction. This allowed what is known here as the poor phenomenon to be given. The common phenomenon is tied, though admittedly in a more complex manner, to what Marion referred to as the "second reduction," insofar as the latter does allow us to be led back to what has the structure of an object and essential differences in ways of Being. The saturated phenomenon and revelation, likewise, are peculiar to what he regards as the third reduction. [13]

The work in *Reduction and Givenness* only brought us to the point of advancing to the so-called "third" reduction, and if the poor and the common phenomena have to be determined on the basis of saturated phenomena, then we need to revisit the issue. However, the treatment of the poor and the common in *Being Given* is nothing less than sparse. This sparseness raises and leaves unanswered many important questions—questions that have to be treated on the basis of the givenness of saturated phenomena or revelation.

3. POVERTY

For the sake of convenience when speaking of phenomena other than saturated ones, let me follow a trend initiated by Marion himself. I will

---

12.   Marion, *Étant donné*, 313–14; Marion, *Being Given*, 224–25.
13.   See Jean-Luc Marion, *Réduction et donation: recherches sur Husserl, Heidegger et la phénoménologie* (Paris: PUF, 1989). English translation as *Reduction and Givenness: Investigations of Husserl, Heidegger, and Phenomenology*, trans. Thomas A. Carlson (Evanston, IL: Northwestern University Press, 1998). Perhaps because he thought he had already treated extensively what became the poor and the common phenomena in *Reduction and Givenness*, he did not feel the need to revisit them in his subsequent work. (Whereas Marion has elaborated upon his notion of the saturated phenomenon, and the exemplary types of saturation, in a separate work, titled *De surcroît*, or *In Excess*, following the publication of *Being Given*.) [Jean-Luc Marion, *De surcroît: études sur les phénomènes saturés* (Paris: PUF, 2001). English translation as *In Excess: Studies of Saturated Phenomena*, trans. Robyn Horner and Vincent Berraud (New York: Fordham University Press, 2002)].

now use the expression "poverty" or "poor" to refer to all types of phenomena that do not give themselves in a revelatory manner. Except for a few instances, Marion will press the poverty of givenness into service so broadly that "poor" comes to designate all those phenomena that give themselves as an object or anything that has the structure of an object. Even the subject, who takes itself as an object, is regarded as "poor."[14]

If we are to determine the poverty of givenness on the basis of revelation, as Marion suggests, then there are on my interpretation at least four types of phenomena that are not saturated phenomena, three of which rightly can be called poor—if we understand by "poverty" that which is not saturated in the manner in which Marion has described. Therefore, under the general rubric of poverty, I want to advance these further distinctions. This will require a critical appropriation of Marion's descriptions, moving into my concept of vertical delimitation. I distinguish between what I term (A) the poor phenomenon proper, (B) the humble phenomenon, (C) the denigrated phenomenon, and (D) pride as the poverty of the gifted.

The question, I will suggest, is whether the "poor phenomenon proper" or the presentational object remains itself *merely* presentational. Can it also not in and through its presentation, de-limit, vertically?

---

14. For example, Marion, *Étant donné*, 354; Marion, *Being Given*, 256: "its [the subject's] mode of apparition remains essentially determined by that of *objectness*. In effect, by being reduced to an 'I think,' the 'subject' is focused on the object, whose presenter and representer it alone becomes by virtue of the essence of representation—to the point that, when it wants to represent itself directly to itself, it has no other possibility but to assume one more time (and one time too many) *the poorest phenomenality— that of the object*" (my emphasis). And Marion, *Étant donné*, 362–63; Marion, *Being Given*, 262–63: "The likely difference between the concepts that Descartes used and those that the contemporary sciences prefer . . . is less important than what they share: the *intuitively poor givenness* realized by the formula, and the quantity and coordinates of the piece of wax, which enable it to be defined but in no way seen. The concept of the wax does not yet show it; its intelligibility does not always phenomenalize it" (my emphasis). Also Marion, *Étant donné*, 419–20; *Being Given*, 305: "But to claim that what is firmly willed should first be conceived in evidence, in short, to claim to know what one wants, one first has to admit that one sees without wanting and before wanting. Now, we know that we *see without wanting only the poorest phenomena*, indeed those that are barely constituted. As soon as a phenomenon is enriched [sic] with intuition, therefore as soon as its degree of givenness grows [sic], it is necessary that we constitute it and bear it for it to be seen, therefore wanted—truly wanted, not denied or evaded. In order to see, one must first want to see" (my emphasis).

A. The Poor Phenomenon Proper

The poor phenomenon proper is the phenomenon of perceptual and epistemic experiences. In and of itself, there is nothing wrong with this kind of givenness. It is what I have called elsewhere "presentation."[15]

Rather than focus on the epistemic object, because Marion has done this with respect to eidetic objects, let me emphasize the passive, perceptual ones. Husserl has described this kind of phenomenon in astonishing detail in his analyses of passive synthesis.[16] Although Marion mentions in passing the phenomenon of passive synthesis in the context of saturation,[17] let me be more precise because aside from some similar characteristics, the passively given affective phenomenon should not be equated with the saturated phenomenon.

Husserl's descriptions concerning the experience of passive synthesis account for the fact that the constitution of meaning, and thus "givenness," is something more than the fulfillment or intuition of the object corresponding to the subjective intention. Sense occurs prior to the activity of the subject, prior to egoic constitution, and prior to judicative acts. Sense emergence is a veritable "constitutive duet," as Husserl terms it. Even when I intend an object or aspect of an object, there is a *plus ultra* of my intention when I discover in the course of perception that there is always more to see, to touch, to smell, or to hear than my active and passive movements of sense-bestowal.[18] It belongs to the structure of the transcendent object to be given in perspectives with referential implications that guide the perceiver.

Moreover, Husserl accounts for the fact that "pre-objects" can exert an affective force on me; they come into "affective relief"; they exert their motivational force on the kinesthetic body, and *they* can lure "me" into *their* active constitution. Husserl even speaks of this in terms of a "call" that resounds from the side of the object itself; the object or object-like formation instigates what I could later anticipate of it.[19]

---

15.   See Steinbock, *Phenomenology and Mysticism*. See also, Steinbock, *Moral Emotions*.

16.   See Edmund Husserl, *Analyses Concerning Passive and Active Synthesis: Lectures on Transcendental Logic*, trans. Anthony J. Steinbock (Dordrecht: Kluwer, 2001), esp. Part 2; hereafter, *Analyses*.

17.   Marion, *Étant donné*, 315; *Being Given*, 226.

18.   Husserl, *Analyses*, 39. Husserl writes that perspectival givenness is so intrinsic to the givenness of a spatial object that even God or a superhuman intellect could not overcome this kind of inadequate givenness. Cf. *Analyses*, 56.

19.   Cf. Husserl, *Analyses*, 43, and Division 3, Part 2.

As much as this may sound like Marion's notion of saturation in some respects, Marion means something else. Saturation has to be more than the passive or active negotiation that occurs between the "subject" and "object." Certainly, we often detect an overflowing of my intention on the part of the object, and even a precedence of the object over the subject. The difference between the former negotiation and saturation, however, consists in the fact that in the case of the latter, activity "falls to the phenomenon and to it alone." "Thus it does indeed show *itself* because it gives *itself* first—in anticipation of every aim, free of every concept, according to a befalling that delivers its self." [20]

The difficulty with Marion's analysis in this regard is that he does not account for the fact that in one respect, the poor phenomenon proper *has its own integrity* as a nonsaturated phenomenon. The poor phenomenon as a perceptual and judicative object should not be something that it is not. But it is always more than what it is; or rather, it is fully itself as it manifests beyond itself, "vertically." [21] The poor phenomenon proper is just the way it gives itself in perceptual and judicative experience. [22] We should not forget that even perceptual and judicative experiences are "genuine" insofar and to the extent that we let them give themselves as they are, which is to say, we do arbitrarily impose limits on them. Perceptual and judicative experiences of perceptual and judicative objects are ways in which we engage the world around us. But is the poor phenomenon thereby "poor"? The poor phenomenon, understood properly as vertically de-limited would be— playing on Marion's terms—the "humble phenomenon." [23] By vertically de-limited, I mean being given specifically (delimited) as it "is," and

---

20. Marion, *Étant donné*, 315; Marion, *Being Given*, 226.
21. For my concept of verticality, see footnote 23 below.
22. Yet there is an obvious ambiguity here concerning eidetic objects and regarding them as "poor" phenomena. On the one hand, what could be richer than the givenness of the essence? Eidetic insight or categorial intuition is a givenness. It is not abstract because for Husserl it is given only through a simple, perceptual, concrete intuition. For Husserl, the categorial is founded in the simple, the concrete. So as a givenness, it is an intuition, and there is a surplus of the categorial over the simple. On the other hand, for the categorial itself to be saturated in Marion's sense, the categorial would have to be founded in the simple such that a simple intuition would (be able to?) overthrow the categorial. I think this is the case with Husserl's notion of the optimal in the phenomenology of normality and abnormality, but this does not make it revelation in the strict sense. This only means it is not a saturated phenomenon. See Anthony J. Steinbock, "Saturated Intentionality," in *The Body: Classic and Contemporary Readings*, ed. Donn Welton (London: Blackwell, 1999), 178–99.
23. For the concept of verticality and de-limitation, see Steinbock, *Phenomenology and Mysticism*, Introduction and Conclusion.

as it "is" opening beyond itself (de-limited), as from beyond itself, in a way that absolute persons or Persons are revealed in the phenomenon.

B. The Humble Phenomenon

Humble phenomena are those phenomena that give themselves with their own (presentational) integrity, but/and in the service of vertical givenness, and qualify that givenness (in my terms) as revelation, manifestation, exposure, display, disclosure. In Marion's schema, that givenness would be "revelation." However, it is difficult for Marion's "saturation" to account for a wide range of religious experiences (from the experiences of St. Francis of Assisi, to Rabbi Dov Baer, to Ruzbīhān Baqlī).[24] We need cite only one example from St. Teresa of Avila's experience to illuminate this point.

When some of her novices were getting disturbed at being drawn away from contemplative prayer to undertake putative menial, mundane tasks, St. Teresa offers the following instruction: "Know that if it is in the kitchen, the Lord walks among the pots and pans helping you both interiorly and exteriorly."[25] My point in making this short remark is that the "pots and pans" are not simply what Marion calls saturated phenomena. Nor are they "poor" or "common" phenomena. Indeed, they are themselves as kitchen utensils, common objects, and they have all the identifiable characteristics of objects. Yet even in their everydayness, there is more, not a quantitative more, but a qualitative opening and reception. For St. Teresa, "even" in the everyday common experience, in the context of use, in the technology of cooking, God is present in the activities involving pots and pans. The pots and pans give themselves in "the epiphany of the everyday," to borrow a phrase from Richard Kearney. True, Marion has accounted for how phenomena reveal, but he has not accounted for how otherwise poor phenomena can remain, on the one hand, "themselves" and, on the other hand, how they *reveal in and through their own proper "poverty"*—which is not

---

24. As Kevin Hart also points out in a different register, the revelation as it takes place on Mt. Sinai to Moses cannot be revelation in Marion's sense because the latter completely excludes the element of the idol. See Kevin Hart, "Torah, God and Idol," in *Ancient Israelite Philosophy*, ed. Alex Kohav, forthcoming.

25. Santa Teresa de Jesús, *Obras Completas*, ed. Efren de La Madre de Dios, O.C.D., and Otger Steggink, O. Carm. (Madrid: Biblioteca de Autores Cristianos, 1997), 690; hereafter, *Obras*. English translation by Kieran Kavanaugh, O.C.D., and Otilio Rodriguez, O.C.D., as *The Collected Works of St. Teresa of Avila* (Washington, DC: ICS Publications, 1985), vol. 3, "Foundations," Section 5.8; hereafter, *Collected Works*.

poverty at all. They simultaneously present themselves and "reveal" what is other than themselves in and through their givenness. This is what I mean in part by vertical de-limitation.

One may argue that this is what Marion means by the saturated phenomenon: for some, the painting calls; for others, it does not. I also realize that Marion is not giving us a list of things that are or are not saturated, but rather, describing a unique *kind of givenness*, for him, simply "revelation." Nonetheless, his descriptions of the poor phenomenon do not give us an account of how poverty can be putative poverty *and* simultaneously reveal. Otherwise, he would not limit the scientific or the technological objects *to the scientific "mathematical" or to the technological, merely*. This would not be de-limitation, but arbitrary limitation. To see these phenomena as de-limiting, he would have to be attentive to the "humble" phenomenon. This de-limitation or in-direction *modifies the very experience itself and the orientation to that particular sphere of experience*. Only with the integration of, say, technology and loving (as the generative movement toward the flourishing of a bearer of value in its own value range as de-limiting) is there the possibility of the redemption of the technical.

The fact that Marion does not treat mathematics or technology (or mathematical and technological objects) as possibly "revealing" in and through their so-called poverty suggests that Marion is limiting the "poor" merely to its putative poverty.

C. The Denigrated Phenomenon

This general givenness and movement of the humble phenomenon I call vertical de-limitation because in its specification as, say, scientific, technological, or utensil, the phenomenon also simultaneously reveals what is more than its epistemic, technological, or useful quality; it opens up "vertically" such that it is not limited to "its own" or better, "one," dimension of experience. Rather than mono-dimensional, it is polyvalent.

The denigrated phenomenon arises when the delimitation or specific orientation of an act or object is *not* simultaneously realized as a de-limitation, when, for example, the technical life is restricted *to the technical sphere merely*, *not* allowing it "to reveal" or "to manifest" or "to expose" or "to display" in a de-limiting manner (i.e., as vertical). In this case, the poverty of the phenomenon is the poverty of experience in the sense that it arbitrarily limits the phenomenon *to itself, merely*. It is

arbitrary because there is no justification to this limitation, when, origi-
narily and fundamentally, it is already de-limiting. Not allowing the
phenomenon to be all it can be, namely, vertical, "revealing" more than
itself in its putative poverty, it denigrates givenness. Denigration, however, can be named as such only from the perspective of verticality.

Cast in the light of Marion's exposition, isn't the denigrated phenomenon, what Marion really means by "poverty," determined from
the essence of saturation? Doesn't Marion really mean by poverty what
we would also have to call the "secularized" phenomenon? After all, if
phenomena can reveal in the strict sense, then cutting revelation short
could not amount to a neutrally given thing. It could never be merely
"poor"; rather, it would suggest an arbitrary deprivation of its ability to
give itself in its verticality. Again, I say "arbitrary" because there are
no grounds for cutting short the givenness. Anything short of verticality
in its fullness is subjectively capricious, namely, the exercise of the
subject over the vertical givenness of the phenomenon. Would this not
have to mean for Marion, the denigration of saturation?

In this case, poverty would not belong to the structure of the object,
but to our deficiency in being ready to receive the givenness, which is
to say, to receive it as saturated. Accordingly, we would have ambiguity at the heart of "poverty": an essential poverty that is peculiar to
every kind of "seeing" and about which I think there is nothing we can
do—which properly speaking could not be called poverty. And we
would have a poverty of self-imposition without reception, in which the
saturated phenomenon as revelation, as call, *is missed.* In this case, it
would not be poverty, but denigration.

But there is also another kind of "poverty" broadly construed—
which is not poverty, but humiliation: one whose violence is more
evident because it denigrates from the start what is properly saturated
(saturated in Marion's sense, but *mutatis mutandis* vertical in my
sense). We need not dwell on this point for my purposes here. It is
enough to evoke the significance of the "face" of the Other who is
regarded merely as an object. In Marion's words, "since intuition always comes after the fact and plays the role of actual confirmation of
the plan's original rationality, and since it should make no difference
('flawless'), it should not tolerate any innovation, modification, or, in
short, any event."[26] The denigrated phenomenon is therefore the vertically de-limiting and de-limited phenomenon creatively, historically,

---

26. Marion, *Étant donné*, 314; Marion, *Being Given*, 225.

restricted in its ability vertically to reveal, manifest, expose, display, disclose.

D. Pride as the Poverty of the Gifted

Staying with Marion, we might ask ourselves how what I have called the denigrated phenomena could arise, how denigration could take shape in the face of revelation. Marion considers this problem with his description of the "responsal" and the "abandon."

The Responsal

The responsal is the process of "admitting" or "wanting" to receive the given. But it is more than that; it is also wanting to receive oneself from the given as given over *to it*. I have to give myself over to the given in order to see. In this way, the responsal transforms what gives itself into what shows itself because it sees nothing of the phenomenon before giving itself over to it.[27]

One could question Marion's problematic invocation of volition here by his use of the expression "wanting." But his point is clear enough: someone who does not dispose herself or himself, who has not made an "immanent decision," will not "see" the given. The putative poor phenomenon, now in our sense of the denigrated phenomenon, is what I see without wanting to see. I see in ordinary terms without receiving, only as constituting it. I master it before I could receive it or "want" to receive it. The problem is not on the "side" of phenomenal givenness, but on the side of the "subject," a subject who has to be understood more precisely in Marion's terms as the gifted.

The Abandon

What is the root of this lack of wanting, this lack of self-disposal, of receiving myself as given, and not allowing what gives itself to show itself? For Marion, the difficulty seems to be almost of neutral, impartial import. For example, Marion writes that "it sometimes happens that what gives itself does not succeed in showing itself" because the monstration of the given takes place "in the essential finitude of the

---

27. Marion, *Étant donné*, 419–20; Marion, *Being Given*, 304–305.

gifted."[28] Because this finitude is essential, and because what gives itself is received only within the finitude of the gifted, it will always be the case that not everything that gives itself, and not all of what gives itself, can show itself. Essentially, the gifted cannot receive the given in the manner in which it gives itself, namely, "without limit or reserve."[29] Notice that this would seem to be a kind of *essential* poverty of the gifted—should this be maintained poverty. For the gifted in the responsal may "want" to receive the given, but essentially (because of our finitude) cannot do so "without limit or reserve."

In distinction, there seems to be yet another kind of poverty of the gifted, one more historically and ethically significant whereby I "want" (or do not "want") to receive the given. Thus, we are faced with the "can/could" of receiving and the "want/would" of receiving. We read: "If the gifted always phenomenalizes what gives itself to him and receives himself from it, nothing establishes that the gifted always *can or wants* to receive *all* that is given." Marion continues that we can never exclude those cases in which a given would not succeed in showing itself "because the gifted *could* or simply *would* not receive it; we can only imagine those unpredictable landings in which the gifted fails before the excess of the given or remains idle in its shortage."[30]

It is helpful for us to distinguish two types of gifted poverty here, the essential and the historical. In effect, however, these are not two different poverties because it is not a matter of choosing or not choosing in any moment of time. We are pushed back, not merely to a historical "immanent decision" of Marion, but to what Derrida has called, drawing on Foucault, "*the* Decision."[31] We are faced with the *decisive* act, that fundamental "point," which is not a point in time, but a "temporal originality in general."[32] In my finitude, I prepare myself or do not prepare myself to receive the given and to be transformed into the gifted.

---

28. Marion, *Étant donné*, 425, 426; Marion, *Being Given*, 309, 310. "The given comes, on its own, upon the gifted, whose structural secondariness attests an absolute finitude."

29. Marion, *Étant donné*, 425; Marion, *Being Given*, 309.

30. Marion, *Étant donné*, 426; Marion, *Being Given*, 310, my emphasis. See also some implications that Lewis draws from this in his introduction, "The Phenomenlogical Concept of Givenness and the 'Myth of the Given,'" in Jean-Luc Marion, *The Reason of the Gift*, trans. Stephen E. Lewis (Charlottesville: University of Virginia Press, 2011), esp. 16–7.

31. See Jacques Derrida, *L'écriture et la différence* (Paris: Seuil, 1967), 62.

32. Derrida, *L'écriture*, 86, fn.: "Il s'agit mois d'un *point* que d'une originarité temporelle en général."

For me, however, the issue is not whether there are "limits" or "reserves," but whether these limits are or are not "de-limiting." " There is something missing in Marion's depiction of the problem, and this is because of the fact that, after all, poverty does not ultimately get determined by him from the standpoint of vertical givenness: epiphany, revelation, manifestation, exposure, disclosure, display (or for him, simply "revelation"). Is it really (i.e., most profoundly) a matter of a "could" or "would" or "idleness"? On the one hand, we have to put it in more appropriate terms, namely, in terms appropriate to verticality. Understood with respect to vertical givenness, there is a "subjective" poverty here that is peculiar to what he calls the gifted: *the poverty of pride*. Pride is to be understood as the clinging to the self, as ultimate self-interest and so (purposefully or not) not allowing the given to show itself. We have to ask: Is the essential finitude just the way things are? Does it point us to the problem of sin as essential finitude, to the Fall? In my terms from *Phenomenology and Mysticism*, this amounts to the problem of idolatry and not a mere "could not/would not" of receiving; it amounts in other terms to "pride": the unmotivated and self-dissimulating self-salience that includes and presupposes others through their exclusion.[33]

Notice that for Marion, the given as it gives itself and the re-qualification of the subject into the gifted are ultimately not within my power. In some sense, "to want" to receive would also be an expression of pride. "What comes after the 'subject,' namely, the gifted, is characterized by the submission of its undeniable activity and live spontaneity to the passivity of an absolutely originary receptivity."[34] In the face of the given, the response (admitting it, etc.) becomes more and more insufficient and therefore endlessly repeated, but more and more fruitful. That is, through the excess of the given over the response, through a given that is more powerful than could have been anticipated, we, "the gifted," become humble in the face of the given—because after all, it's not about the gift. The gifted receives and thereby receives itself.[35]

It will be necessary eventually to requalify the gifted as the *beloved* (as "given" through the *revelation* of loving).[36] But for now let me ask: Can we or to what extent can we (actively) submit our activity to passivity? Can *we* accomplish the self-denial and attenuation of the self

---

33. See Steinbock, *Moral Emotions*, Chapter 1.
34. Marion, *Étant donné*, 425–26; Marion, *Being Given*, 310.
35. Marion, *Étant donné*, 420–21, 424; Marion, *Being Given*, 305–6, 308.
36. In Steinbock, *Loving, Hating, and the Beloved*, forthcoming.

so that what gives itself can show itself? Or instead, cannot the self-disposal be accomplished only by an "other" whom I serve? Is it not by being occupied by another—in religious experience, by God; in moral experience, by the other person; in aesthetic experience, by, for example, the dance or the sand castle at the beach—that the self is called into question, and only in this way? Is there perhaps something we can do to dispose ourselves to allow what gives itself to show itself, or in other words, to rescind the Decision? In my view, this would have to take place through a different kind of poverty, what the mystics call the *"poverty of spirit."*[37]

Thus, we encounter one more distinction that is made by nearly all the mystics of the Abrahamic tradition, the distinction between what can be accomplished by virtue of our own efforts and what can be received only as a gift or in an "infused" manner. Marion does hint at the latter, though not in these terms. He writes of "a given that accomplishes itself on the basis of its irreducible self, therefore one that sometimes . . . is not governed by the receptive capacity of the gifted and thus frees itself of these limits." In other words, for me (as I attempt to show in a subsequent work), it is a matter of *loving* that alone can exceed the "limits and reserves" of the gifted whether the gifted can/could, want to/would receive.

CONCLUSION

I introduced Marion's concept of the "poor phenomenon" in distinction to his concept of the saturated phenomenon, and I suggest that the phenomenon of the "poor" is not the poverty of the phenomenon at all. In fact, it is properly to be understood as what I call the "humble phenomenon." The humble phenomenon is fully itself, but as itself, opens or is de-limited, vertically exposing, revealing, manifesting, displaying, disclosing, vertical dimensions of reality. Loving, which accepts what is given, but is generative beyond the given as a non-violent invitational, improvising movement or force, is the most profound expression of this vertical de-limiting movement.

---

37. St. Teresa writes, for example, "I fear that it [the soul] will never attain true poverty of spirit, which means being at rest in labors and dryness and not seeking consolation or comfort in prayer—for earthly consolation has already been abandoned—but seeking consolation in trials for love of Him who always lived in the midst of them." *Obras*, 124; *Collected Works* (1976), vol. 1, Section 22.11. See Steinbock, *Phenomenology and Mysticism*.

The phenomenon restricted and limited merely to itself, by contrast, is to be understood as the denigrated phenomenon. This is because of the poverty of the gifted, namely, what I call here the poverty of pride. In my view, if we are to speak of poverty at all, then it should be in the way the mystics use the term, namely, the poverty of spirit as an opening to the opening, or more personally, the vertical de-limitation accomplished through loving.

In the final chapter of this work, Chapter 5, I resituate the problem of the gift, giving, and givenness in a description of gift-giving provided by Maimonides. This is a historical step backward, but a phenomenological step forward. It is a historical step backward because much of our discussions concerning the gift have been spurred by contemporary analyses, including Jacques Derrida's critiques of the economy of the gift and Marion's "reduction" of the gift in his phenomenology of givenness. But it is a step forward because Maimonides describes a dimension of gift-giving that is not characterized explicitly in these contemporary discussions, although it is essential to them.

In Chapter 5, I briefly examine Jacques Derrida's exposition of the gift and then turn to Marion's threefold reduction. After articulating Maimonides's delineation of gift-giving, I argue that his portrayal of the gift and gift-giving contributes to the contemporary debate by suggesting that is not about the gift at all; rather, it concerns participating with others toward their liberation.[38]

---

38. This chapter originally appeared with some variation as "The Poor Phenomenon: Marion and the Problem of Givenness," *Alter: revue de phénoménologie* 15 (2007), 357–72.

Chapter 5

Resituating the Gift in Maimonides

Participation and Liberation

I have tried to show the different ways in which the gift does not become a gift by being surprising, by demanding a retreat of the giver, by being abandoned to a transcendent manifestation that induces amnesia, or by being reduced to a superior form of "revelatory" givenness. This final chapter is an attempt to resituate the gift through which it can show itself as such. It goes from the dimension of mere gift-giving to the dynamic of our participation with other persons.

To make this move, I briefly recap Jacques Derrida's critique of the gift as it appears in the economy of giving, and then I examine Marion's determination of the gift described in his phenomenology of givenness. This will help to highlight the unique contribution made by Maimonides's delineation of gift-giving. Taking these steps will also help to clarify a deeper sense of the gift than is often considered in "ontological," post-modernist, or so-called phenomenological treatments and to resituate the gift and gift-giving in its proper context—suggested in different ways through this work—in interpersonal relations as participating with others.

1. DECONSTRUCTION OF THE PURE GIFT: DERRIDA

Spurred by an original reading of Marcel Mauss on the potlatch and the gift, Jacques Derrida claims that the gift is not merely factually impossible, but it is the very meaning of the impossible, which is to say, it is impossible for the gift to appear as such and still remain the gift. This is because, for the gift to be realized as such, it must annul itself *as* gift. Put differently, if a gift is "present," the circumstances that were required for a gift to be a gift have made the gift vanish in the moment of its realization.[1]

How is this the case? For Derrida, a gift and the process of gift-giving require that someone give something to someone else: to the gift belongs an intention of giving and an intention toward a gift. Further, whether or not I mean for this to happen, the gift motivates a counter-gift in the form of an obligation, a demand, or a debt (even if in the form of gratitude or thankfulness, such as "I owe you a debt of thanks"). The gift, therefore, whether or not I want it to, can be a form of control over or domination of another. The moment the gift appears to another as gift, when it takes on the meaning of gift, it becomes part of the economic structure, a circulation of exchange in the circle of debt and narcissistic gratitude.[2] It then gets canceled out or destroyed as gift and cannot appear as such. Therefore, it is impossible for the gift to appear as such. This is not to say that "there is" no gift; rather, if there is a gift, it must be the experience of the impossible. Accordingly, the gift "as such" is impossible; it is not merely an impossible experience, but the experience of the impossible.[3]

The network of meanings of the gift are such that I do not have "to want" the gift to have these implications; they are intrinsic to the gift itself. For example, I may give a gift because I want more in return, like an investment. Or I may give up something now to another because I expect to capitalize on it later (from practicing an instrument to a possession in a board game). However, I may give a gift, but want *nothing in return*. Lewis Hyde shows in his wonderful reflections on the gift that even when an exchange is not explicit, even if it perishes for those

---

1. Jacques Derrida, *Donner le temps: 1. La fausse monnaie* (Paris: Galilée, 1991), 18–9, 24. English translation by Peggy Kamuf, *Given Time: 1. Counterfeit Money*, vol. 1 (Chicago, University of Chicago Press, 1992), 7, 12. See Marcel Mauss, "Essai sur le don. Forme et raison de l'échange dans les societes archaïques," *Sociologie et anthropologie* (Paris: PUF, 1989/1950). Marcel Mauss, *The Gift: The Form and Reason for Exchange in Archaic Societies*, trans. W. D. Halls (New York: W. W. Norton & Company, 2000).

2. See Derrida, *Donner le temps*, 38; Derrida, *Given Time*, 23.

3. See the dialogue between Derrida and Marion, "On the Gift," in *God, the Gift, and Postmodernism*, ed. John D. Caputo and Michael J. Scanlon (Bloomington, IN: Indiana University Press, 1999), 54–78.

who give it away, even as anonymous or indirect, and even if it has the power to unite (a point I take up in the conclusion), there is an essential "gift cycle," a circle of exchange, commerce—in short, a return.[4] For Derrida, the insight is that the gift itself, its very structure, imposes an obligation on the other to "return," even if only "*to give* thanks." Even to say "don't thank me" already presupposes on my part the circulation of the gift and the debt of thanks. "Paying it forward" instead of "paying it back" would involve the same dynamic, only under a different name.

Moreover, although I may think my gift to another is given freely, it never occurs ex nihilio; Derrida would maintain that it originates from some prior motivation. It may be just a wish to give a gift to express my gratitude; it may be "just because." But even this "just because" relies on a prior motivation. In fact, if someone were to give something to me completely unmotivated—and let's suppose that I do not even know the person!—I could immediately ask why he or she is giving this to me: "OK, what do you want from me?" or I may think to myself "What's behind his intention?" These are just some examples that articulate how the very conditions of the possibility of the gift constitute, for Derrida, an economy of exchange.

Yet the pure gift, the very essence of the gift, what something has to be in order to be a gift, for Derrida, must *interrupt* all economy, all exchange. To be a gift, it must escape all motivation and all intention, all anticipation, all "present" and all fulfillment; to be "gift" in its pure essential sense *as* gift, it must be able to arise unprovoked, unbidden, unannounced, unreceived, unattended. To be gift, it must be free from anticipation. I cannot very well say "Pay attention now; here comes a pure gift" and keep it outside of the economy of the gift. In fact, the aporia that Derrida notes, what makes the gift impossible to appear as such, is that for the gift to be a gift, it can never be noticed as such by anyone. And isn't this non-sensical situation the very "figure of impossibility," namely, that to be a gift as such, it cannot appear as such, in principle, it cannot be noticed by anyone as gift? What would be the point? Yet to be and to remain a gift, and not to incite a counter-gift, it must not even appear as gift. This indeed seems to be another way of characterizing sheer emergence, "sheer eventing," like we witnessed in

---

4. Lewis Hyde, *The Gift: Creativity and the Artist in the Modern World* (New York: Vintage Books, 2007), for instance, 19–20, 23, 103, 115, 148, 196–97, 211.

the case of Heidegger and *Ereignis* peculiar to the "It" gives, the sheer emergent "Taking Place."

Let me continue. Not only can the gift not be the unnoticed, it has to be the immemorial in the sense that it has to have been already forgotten. I have to be forgetful of the gift before it could be present and retained for it to remain outside of any possibility of exchange or return—any gift-intention, real or imputed. Such a forgetfulness must interrupt the gift as "present" and then as a retained present. A retained present, a retention, which is the immediate and unassailable [*undurchstreibar*] lingering of the present, would always be available to be "present" and thus to demand a return, even if in the form of thanks or as a rebuttal (why me?). Thus, for the gift to appear as gift, it cannot merely be repressed in memory, ignored, or forgotten (which again would still be retained as a "present" that is not present); instead, it must take place in an *absolute forgetfulness* of the gift such that the gift "appears" only in the annulment of any circumstance in which it could appear as gift. In this way, the pure gift, "if there is any," becomes the condition of absolute forgetting.[5] The pure gift in principle can never be "pure" or "innocent" because its very meaning is to be within the economy of exchange and rupture the economy of exchange; in fact, the gift realizes this economy in the rupture of this economy. For Derrida, the gift, therefore, "if there is any," is the figure of the impossible. And thus, for a gift to appear as gift, it would have "to appear" nonsensically without past, without present, without future, without meaning, without context, without witness.[6] Or again, it would have to be akin to the sheer eventing of Heidegger's "*Ereignis ereignet*," "taking place takes place" that I described in Chapter 2.

Now, there are a variety of questions and objections that one could pose at this stage, and there are some issues of concern that I address later in this chapter. The latter concern the reduction of different modes of givenness to one predominate mode of givenness, the quality of interpersonal relations, and different emotions peculiar to persons in which the structure of such an "economy" is not given and does not

---

5. Derrida, *Donner le temps*, 29–31, 119; Derrida, *Given Time*, 16–18, 91.

6. See Jacques Derrida's interpretation of the "evil genius" in Descartes, *L'écriture et la différence* (Paris: Seuil, 1967), esp. 78–96; Jacques Derrida, *Writing and Difference*, trans. Alan Bass (Chicago: University of Chicago Press, 1978), esp. 50–62. It would be interesting to discover where "giving birth" would fit in Derrida's analyses—an example that Derrida to the best of my knowledge does not use. It does not seem that it would fall into an essential economy of exchange.

structure the experience.[7] For my purposes, however, I want to turn again to Marion, but this time as he explicitly treats the matter of the gift in relation to Derrida. For Marion, what Derrida deems impossible and the figure of the impossible shows only that what Derrida analyzed in no way deserves the name "gift."[8] Thus, although for Derrida, all relations of the gift are economic in some way, for Marion there are some relations that are not economic. Because Marion appropriates Derrida in his own interpretation of the gift and the gifted, let me not dwell further on Derrida's critique of the economy of giving and the gift—which describes it as the figure of the impossible—but move directly to Marion. Marion assumes Derrida's critique of the economy of the gift, but goes one step further by bracketing the economic movement to get at the meaning or sense of the gift, the giver, and the givee—to get at givenness itself.[9]

2. REDUCTION OF THE GIFT: MARION

Before discussing the non-economic ways in which the gift can be a gift, I want to acknowledge that prior to his later explicit reflections on the gift and givenness, Marion did sketch a reply to Heidegger's understanding of Being, the gift, onto-theology, and implicitly, I venture to say, his esotericism—intended or unintended. Marion did this especially in his *God without Being* and his emphasis on loving as agape or divine giving—which gives (itself)—in which God does not fall within

---

7. See Steinbock, *Moral Emotions.*
8. See Derrida, *Donner le temps,* 24–26, 42; Derrida, *Given Time,* 12–4, 27. See Marion, *Étant donné,* 118–24; Marion, *Being Given,* 80–85.
9. See John D. Caputo and Michael J. Scanlon, ed., *God, the Gift, and Postmodernism* (Bloomington, IN: Indiana University Press, 1999). See, for example, the thorough study, Jason W. Alvis, *Marion and Derrida on The Gift and Desire: Debating the Generosity of Things* (Dordrecht: Springer, 2016). In the context of critical theory, see Romand Coles, *Rethinking Generosity: Critical Theory and the Politics of Caritas* (Ithaca: Cornell University Press, 1997).

the realm of Being, but comes to us in and as "gift."[10] However, this does not yet explicitly reply to Derrida where the possibility of the gift is concerned, even though, as John Maraldo carefully points out, Marion's treatment of the phenomenology of the gift in his later work is another way of carrying out and clarifying Marion's earlier attempt to free God (as crossed out)—in which all the components of God as gift are bracketed—from the onto-theological determination of God as Being/being.[11] Let me turn to these issues now.

Rather than dismissing Derrida's study, Marion is able to advance to a next stage of analysis thanks to his (Derrida's) observations, in particular, observations concerning the contradictions generated by presupposing the transcendent conditions of the gift. It is the problem of *givenness*, for Marion, and more specifically different orders or ways of givenness, which open the way to a phenomenological analysis of the gift.

Marion undertakes a threefold "epochē" or bracketing of the transcendent conditions of economic exchange. This ushers in an attempt to describe the gift as gift without necessarily restricting it to the dynamic of reciprocity and the economy of exchange.[12] He attempts to accomplish this by reducing phenomenologically the gift to givenness and givenness to itself. This reduction entails the threefold bracketing of transcendencies, or the transcendent conditions of exchange, by holding in abeyance the reality of the givee, the giver, and the gift.[13]

Another way of putting this is that for Marion it is necessary to leave the "natural attitude" (Derrida) and move to a phenomenological perspective (Marion) when addressing the gift. Accordingly, bracketing

---

10. Jean-Luc Marion, *Dieu sans l'être* (Paris: PUF, 1991); Jean-Luc Marion, *God without Being*, trans. David Tracy (Chicago: Chicago University Press, 1991), 3, 46–7, 106. Further, on the relation between Marion and Nishida, see the excellent comparative work by John Maraldo, "Nothing Gives: Marion and Nishida on Gift-giving and God," in *Japanese and Continental Philosophy: Conversations with the Kyoto School*, ed. Bret W. Davis, Brian Schroeder, and Jason M. Wirth (Bloomington, IN: Indiana University Press, 2011), 141–59. See also Marion's reflections in the first three chapters of *The Reason of the Gift*, trans. Stephen E. Lewis (Charlottesville: University of Virginia Press, 2011), 19–68. For my part, I focus here on the way in which the gift emerges as gift through the emotional sphere, specifically, through humility and loving, and in this context through interpersonal participation toward liberation.

11. See Maraldo, "Nothing Gives," 148–50.

12. Marion, *Étant donné*, 120, 122–23; *Being Given*, 82, 84.

13. "The objection itself would open onto the response: the gift is reduced to givenness and givenness to itself once the givee, the giver, and the objectivity of the gift are bracketed, thereby detaching the gift from economy and manifesting it according to givenness purified of all cause." Marion, *Étant donné*, 122; *Being Given*, 84.

the empirical trancendencies (or reality or being) of the givee, the giver, and the gift requires neither asserting nor denying the transcendencies of the givee, giver, and gift.[14] In principle, the analyses should entail the phenomenological reduction of transcendence to my lived-experience of the givee, the giver, and the gift to show the gift without reciprocity and exchange.[15] This is because, for Marion, the gift does not name the impossible if and when we treat the gift under its own proper "conditions," its own unique structures of "being given," and if and when we "reduce" the gift phenomenologically to being given.

Bracketing the Givee

Because the givee might be seen as the cause of the gift, and therefore registered in the economy of the gift, Marion begins by bracketing the reality of the givee so that the gift might present itself outside of this exchange. Bracketing the causal efficacy of the givee, Marion homes in on the essence of givenness such that one must always give as if the givee never had to repay, and in which the givee is incapable of reciprocity.[16] What is then my lived-experience of such a "givee"? What is its sense? Marion suggests three ways in which the phenomenality of the givee appears to me in gift-giving. Where the givee is bracketed, the givee, "reduced," appears *as* humanitarian, *as* enemy, and *as* ingrate, correlative to the experiences of giving vis-à-vis anonymity, hostility, and ingratitude.[17] Thus, even without the givee (as a transcendent reality), the gift is accomplished.[18]

Bracketing the Giver

Marion continues this exercise of bracketing by "reducing" the empirical reality of giver to its meaning within givenness. This *epochē* sug-

---

14. See, for example, Marion, *Étant donné*, 135; *Being Given*, 94. Simply asserting non-existence of transcendencies in the place of transcendencies would only count as an uncritical reversal. This is a point, however, that often gets obscured in Marion's analyses, for example, when he wants to entertain the gift "without" the giver, "without" the givee, etc. (passim).

15. See Marion, *Étant donné*, 129; *Being Given*, 89.

16. Marion, *Étant donné*, 124–27; *Being Given*, 85–87.

17. Marion, *Étant donné*, 130–31; *Being Given*, 89–91. Thus, as an example, the "enemy" is incapable of reciprocity. So really, we are involved in a double reduction: (1) the reduction of the givee to the enemy and (2) the reduction of enemy—not to someone I hate—but to the meaning of "incapable of reciprocity."

18. Even the eschatological status of the givee, where the recipient is absent in the world, allows the gift to appear as such; see Derrida and Marion, "On the Gift," 62.

gests that there can still be the gift "without" the empirical reality of the giver being presupposed. Marion provides three examples in which the sense of gift is still maintained while the objective reality of the giver is not at issue. The first case is that of inheritance in which the giver is empirically absent; indeed, here the giver had no intention that the givee repay that which was bequeathed. This second "reduction" according to Marion is evident not only when the giver is unknown to the givee, but also when (say) I, as giver, am unknown to myself as giver. I may (as giver) be unconscious of the giving, for example, when something is given without any intention of giving (I may put something on the sidewalk as garbage, just to get rid of it) or something is taken as a gift without I, as giver, ever knowing or intending anything of the sort. (We have all had the experience of being thanked for something and replying spontaneously "For what?") A third perspective on bracketing the giver yields the experience of indebtedness. The recognition of debt, the obligation through the gift-given, confirms for Marion the recognition of the absent giver in the gift. Not only does it make the indebted essentially the givee; it also produces the impossibility of repayment because the givee as indebted cannot repay anything to anyone. In this way, indebtedness also confirms the possibility of gift without exchange. In sum, the essential character of the gift comes to the fore as "to be received by the givee to whom it appears."[19]

Bracketing the Gift

The third movement of considering gift-giving outside of the economy of exchange entails discerning the meaning of the gift where the gift is not the transfer of an object. For example, I can give my word, I can give power, I can give in person (i.e., myself) to the Other.[20] Here, he maintains, no "thing" is given. After describing the ways in which the gift does not have to coincide with any particular object or with the exchange of an object, Marion discerns two characteristics that define the character of the gift, or better, the lived-experience of the "reduced" gift from the perspectives of both the giver and the givee: For the giver, it is the giveability of the gift; for the givee, it is the receivability or the acceptability of the gift.[21]

---

19. Marion, *Étant donné*, 136–43; *Being Given*, 95–100.
20. Marion, *Étant donné*, 149–51; *Being Given*, 104–5.
21. Marion, *Étant donné*, 154–55; *Being Given*, 108.

On the one hand, according to Marion, the giver is not the starting point of the gift, pure and simple, because the giver decides to give only because he or she yields to "giveability," which is to say, realizes that another gift already obliged him or her. In what Marion calls the realm of the reduction, the situation is such that a "decision of the gift" or a giveability "decides," in fact, "demands" the giver to give: "In deciding the giver to give it, the gift gives itself of itself." Accordingly, the gift is taking place outside of reciprocity because the gift comes from giving itself.

Similarly, when I receive a gift, this is not phenomenologically the transfer of property, nor can it be equated with receiving an object. Instead, it consists phenomenologically in the acceptance, or again, the *acceptability* of the gift, even if the real object is refused or ignored.[22] Thus, acceptability or receivablity means being obliged by the gift and being exposed (and receptive) to its unpredictability as not in my control. In fact, a different temporality is in play, for I "expect" nothing, but only respond to the demand of givenness. It is therefore not the giver who exercises control over the givee, but the gift that obliges the givee as acceptability.[23] Accordingly, giveability and receivability or acceptance show the meaning of the gift without the exchange of an object.

Marion contends, likewise, that "sacrifice" gives the gift back to givenness from which it proceeds "by returning it to the very return that originally constitutes it"—repeating the gift on the basis of its origin— or allowing recognition of the giver, and in this way, the recognition of the whole process of givenness.[24] Thus, sacrifice lets appear the process of givenness itself. Forgiveness too re-gives the gift, but starting from the giver, "who confirms it in the light of givenness for the salvation of the recipient." It too, like sacrifice, lets appear the phenomenality of givenness, but as a redounding of the gift from the giver.[25]

On the whole, then, the gift reduced to givenness is seen as possible precisely when the trancendencies usually associated with gift-giving (the giver, the givee, and the gift) are bracketed so as to reveal their internal sense. Although we might question whether and to what extent the account in *Being Given* really amounts to a phenomenological bracketing or a phenomenological reduction in the strict sense, I want

---

22. Marion, *Étant donné*, 155–56; *Being Given*, 109.
23. Marion, *Étant donné*, 159–61; *Being Given*, 111–13.
24. See above, Chapter 1.
25. Marion, *The Reason of the Gift*, 83–84.

to accept Marion's descriptions in order to turn to the matter of gift-giving in the context of Maimonides's thought.

3. GIFT-GIVING AS PARTICIPATION WITH OTHERS AND LIBERATION: MAIMONIDES

Maimonides, Rabbi Moshe ben Maimon, or as he is also known from the acronym of his name, the Rambam (1138–1204), is the prodigious Jewish philosopher renowned for his multi-volume commentary on the Torah, the *Mishneh Torah*. He is more commonly recognized as the author of the *Guide for the Perplexed* and is frequently cited for his unique laws of *tzedakah* (charity, gift-giving, but also "righteousness" and "justice"). They are distinctive in our context because these laws and orderings of *tzedakah* pertain to giving and to the gift. More specifically and importantly, they are delineated within the context of giving—here, to the poor. This has two important implications for this work. First, giving and the gift admit of degrees, and Maimonides is attentive to these subtleties and nuances of gift-giving; it is not an all or nothing affair. Second, the modes of gift-giving have an interpersonal significance from the very start. This is something that can get lost in the figures examined here: Marion's "bracketing"—to say nothing of Heidegger's "It" gives, and even Henry's revelatory self-affection.

According to Maimonides, there are eight distinctive levels of *tzedakah*, or gift-giving.[26] These distinctive levels (taking up a little more than a printed page) are outlined in his book concerning agriculture (of several hundred pages). Why would such an important topic be couched in a work on agriculture and not in a treatise, say, on spiritual practices or ethical conduct? It is in part because Maimonides is dealing with "seeds" of all kinds, of planting, harvesting, and offering crops. It concerns those who harvest and those who receive; when the land should yield and when it should rest, as in a Sabbatical year; when debts are forgiven; when the corners of the field, or what is dropped while gathering, should be left to the poor; and so on. To facilitate the reader in my interpretation of this text and for the sake of convenience,

---

26. *The Code of Maimonides, Book Seven: The Book of Agriculture*, trans. Isaac Klein (New Haven, CT: Yale University Press, 1979), Chapter 10: 7–14.

I provide in a note the eight degrees of *tzedakah*, that is, the short delineation upon which I comment.[27]

For the purposes of my exposition, allow me to reverse the Rambam's ordering: Whereas he describes them from highest to lowest, I

---

27. The translation offered here by Issac Klein is slightly altered.

[1] 7. There are eight degrees of *tzedakah*, each one superior to the other. The highest degree, than which there is none higher, is one who upholds the hand of an Israelite reduced to poverty by handing him a gift or a loan, entering into a partnership with him, or finding work for him, in order to strengthen his hand, so that he would have no need to beg from other people. Concerning such a one Scripture says, *Thou shalt uphold him; as a stranger and a settler shall he live with thee* (Lev. 25:35), meaning uphold him, so that he would not lapse into want.

[2] 8. Below this is he who gives *tzedakah* to the poor in such a way that he does not know to whom he has given, nor does the poor man know from whom he has received. This constitutes the fulfilling of a *mitzvah* for its own sake, such as the Chamber of Secrets in the Temple, whereunto the righteous would contribute secretly, and wherefrom the poor of good families would draw their sustenance in equal secrecy. Close to such a person is he who gives of *tzedakah* directly to the *kupah* [community fund]. One should not, however, give of *tzedakah* directly to the *kupah* unless he knows that the person in charge of it is trustworthy, is a Sage, and knows how to manage it properly, as was the case of Rabbi Chanania ben Teradion.

[3] 9. Below this is he who knows to whom he is giving, while the poor person does not know from whom he is receiving. He is thus like the great among the Sages who were wont to set out secretly and throw the money down at the doors of the poor. This is a proper way of doing it, and a preferable one if those in charge of *tzedakah* do not conduct themselves as they should.

[4] 10. Below this is the case where the poor person knows from whom he is receiving, but himself remains unknown to the giver. He is thus like the great among the Sages who used to place the money in the fold of a linen sheet which they would throw over their shoulder, whereupon the poor would come behind them and take the money without being ashamed [or exposed to humiliation].

[5] 11. Below this is to give to the poor person directly with one's own hand [into his hand] before being asked.

[6] 12. Below this is to give to the poor person after being asked.

[7] 13. Below this is to give him less than what is proper [inadequately], but with a friendly countenance [gladly with a smile].

[8] 14. Below this is to give with a frowning countenance [begrudgingly].

reorient them in my exposition from lowest to highest. I further group them into three categories (these are my own, and not Maimonides's): (1) those that conform to the economy of the gift, (2) those that are expressive of the bracketing of the gift, and (3) a style of gift-giving that goes beyond each of the former and is expressive of the dynamic of loving, issuing from what we could call the interpersonal nexus of beloveds. Let me also note that it is not the case that these different kinds of giving build on each other or subtract something from the other; rather, they constitute special manners of giving, and they are ordered in terms of their value by the Rambam. What unites them all as giving is their interpersonal connection, participating with another through giving toward a possible liberation from material and/or spiritual restrictions.

Gift-Giving and the Economy of the Gift

Let me first examine those kinds of gift-giving that conform to the economy of the gift. They number four. Here, Maimonides describes a lowest level of giving and the gift. Such a process of gift-giving takes place when one gives, but gives unwillingly and, so to speak, does so resentfully, with a frowning countenance. One implication here is that I experience myself in giving, as giving, such that there is (still) a *self-awareness* in and of giving.[28] The danger is that "I" would be an issue, if not *the* issue: "I" might be the concern of "my" giving. Another implication is that I somehow convey this begrudging quality of my giving to the other and potentially make the other uncomfortable (through a hesitant gesture, a frown, a rigid posture). Even though there is self-consciousness in this giving, it is not purely subjective or interior; but my attitude is or can be felt by another.

Perhaps I feel guilty in this kind of annoyed giving; perhaps I feel that I must reciprocate; perhaps it is the mere sentiment of obligation or duty that governs the action; perhaps another is forcing me to give. In short, for my purposes, although there is indeed a giving, it is attached to compulsion to give and maybe to reciprocate. Within the context of the earlier discussion of Derrida, this kind of gift-giving would find itself within an economy of exchange and, needless to say for Derrida, would not constitute the gift as such.

---

28. See also, Dobh Baer of Lubavitch, *Tract on Ecstasy*, trans. Louis Jacobs (London: Vallentine Mitchell, 1963), 128.

The next level, a bit higher, as it were, is when one gives gladly, kindly, and with a smile but gives inadequately. Two aspects distinguish this kind of giving from the previous one. First, resentment does not accompany the giving, as in the former case. Second, this giving opens the door to the prospect of adequation, specifically, to the prospect of an adequate giving and an adequate gift; it presupposes that there is an intention of giving that does have a complete fulfillment, or a fulfillment that could accomplish completely the intention of giving. In the former case, either adequation is assumed, or it is not at all an issue; instead, it is my resentfulness and possibly making another feel uncomfortable or put off that is the main issue. In this instance, however, the specter of measurement is raised, and I fall short of adequacy.

For whom is the gift-giving inadequate, we may ask? We can assume that Maimonides has in mind an inadequacy vis-à-vis the recipient. But the inadequacy could befall the giver as well. For example, as a parent, I feel that I should always give more, though my children may think that they have already received too much. Maybe I think, subjectively, that there is something that the other person deserves; maybe I sense, objectively, that the other has a need that should be fulfilled, and in either case, it is "less than I could or should do," or it is less than it could be.

Thus, the issue of adequacy and my actual inadequate giving is one issue. For this to be the case, we would have to presuppose the idea of a true reciprocity of intention and fulfillment (in which there is a shortfall now, even though I do it with a friendly countenance). There is an idea of ideal fulfillment in relationship to which the gift-giving is inadequate, though I do not give begrudgingly. Indeed, if this idea were not posited, how could I or the other experience it as inadequate?

But there is still a deeper point—suggested above. It is not that there is some kind of inadequacy in my gift-giving, but at root, this kind of gift-giving assumes that it is *susceptible to measurement*. We may ask as a kind of a marker: Just what kind of giving could be measured? Does giving not in its very nature follow what the mystics might call the movement of holiness, which is beyond measure? Does the essence of giving admit of a limit to giving in relation to which it would be gauged adequate or inadequate?

No matter how we are able to respond to these questions eventually, it is possible to assert here that this kind of gift-giving falls within what Derrida has determined as the economy of the gift. In different ways, depending upon their type, they are susceptible or exposed to an economy of exchange. At the very least, it is not the deepest sense of gift-giving.

Higher than the last, but remaining within an economy of giving, is when one gives—presumably adequately—but only after first being asked to do so. It is not that giving adequately (whatever that might be, and if it is even possible) is not good, but that in this structure of gift-giving, we have the sense that the gift is placed into a requirement of giving. Because I do it after I am asked, in some sense this means that I am not so disposed to the other person that I would think of it on my own! My insensitivity to the position of the other person at root means that I force the other into having to ask. In this case, a different moment is emphasized in relation to the earlier ones. It is not a matter of giving begrudgingly and maybe making the other feel awkward, to say nothing of contributing to my own subjective poor disposition; it is not a matter of giving inadequately but with a smile; rather, I put the other person in a position of having to request, and his or her possible shame makes this shameful.

Of course, when I am writing of gift-giving here for Maimonides, I do not restrict the gift to the transfer of a possession or to something that I may have in my pockets. There is not merely a giving of what I have. One could ask for comforting words, for a good ear to listen, and so on.[29] Further, I do not have to have been asked directly by the person to whom I give; a request could be issued through a friend of a friend of a friend. And if this is the case, then I may never know the direct source!

Let's agree that it is good that I give, even in this case of having to be asked. The point here is that this kind of gift-giving is constrained by a constraint I place on the other to request before I give. We do not have to assume that I could ever anticipate a demand. In fact, it might be endemic to our human finitude and our position before another that we are always already thrown off guard. The point for Maimonides seems to be that this kind of gift-giving constitutes a unique kind of giving that has its own structure; it is not a matter that "we could do better," but rather, that it does not constitute the deepest essence of gift-giving.

To situate this within the context of the discussion at hand, let me suggest that although there is at least a response, an answer of some sort, the response is governed and circumscribed by a constraint on the

---

29. *The Code of Maimonides, Book Seven*, 90.

gift placed on it by a request coming from some other. Even if it were to be counted as a deeper kind of giving than the preceding, this one still succumbs in a different way to Derrida's critique of a gift because responding in this way would for him fall within the economy of exchange.

Lastly, within this first group, and thus still succumbing to the economy of giving, is the case where one gives to the poor person directly, but gives before being asked. The former mode and this one are characterized, in part, in terms of their temporality. In the former case, it is a matter of gift-giving *after* one is asked; in this case, it is a matter of gift-giving *before* one is asked. But the temporal consideration is not the only one involved here. The fact that it is listed only fourth from the bottom and not at the top should provide some indication that simply giving before one is asked does not constitute for Maimonides the deepest kind of giving.

What makes this mode "higher" or a "deeper" form of giving is not merely the fact of giving before one is asked. For Maimonides, I believe, it has the additional component of dealing with the other person *directly.* In my view, this is one aspect that makes it its own form and "higher."

But anticipating the further delineation of gift-giving, why—we might ask—is this very component of directly encountering the other in the gift "with his own hand"—not near the very top or more precisely, right at the top of giving for Maimonides? Why does he place it fourth from the bottom?

The matter does not fully lie in the fact that the person may have her hand out, although not asking verbally. Could she not still be asking without asking? Thus, it could remain a lower form of giving—though giving nonetheless—because I "only" give by beating the other to the punch; I give before she could ask. It could also lead to the experience of pride: "I am doing this before you even asked; what a wonderful giver I am!" This could itself be expressive of a contorted sense of sacrifice. As Marion points out in another context, I may want to rid myself of a possession by destroying it for myself (and for others) and in this way become free of it. But, in making a sacrifice of goods, I may also be demonstrating my autarchy and autonomy to others (and/or to myself).[30] I not only give because I can afford it; I give "till it hurts" to prove myself.

But there is something still more. Implied in this form of giving is that by anticipating the request and fulfilling it in one fell swoop—though I may be dealing with the other person directly, hand to hand—I introduce another temporal component: *I am fulfilling or terminating* my implied obligation in and through the act of gift-giving. Implied here is thus a threshold or a limit placed on giving, even when I do in fact accomplish something. My accomplishment is a finite giving in the sense that I do nothing more than terminate my obligation without having to be asked twice. Thus, it is possible to give in this instance, but to do so *to stop further involvement* with someone. I do not owe or no longer owe anything to anyone; the loss of the object is the loss of interpersonal connection and, in a curious way, the preservation of the self. It closes down immediately what is otherwise a movement of opening up. Accordingly, we could give, not simply to assuage guilt, but to prevent any further contact with the other person. This is why, in my view, such a process or level of giving remains within the economy of exchange and, in any case, remains of the lower sort for the Rambam.

The Reduction of Giving and the Reduced Gift

The next section of giving and of the gift for Maimonides enters the field of what Marion might regard as the reduction of giving and the "reduced" gift, which were treated above. These, in Maimonides's delineation, number three.

Within this set, the first level concerns what Marion identifies as the bracketing of the givee. For Maimonides, this next higher level is expressed when one does not know to whom one gives, but the recipient, the givee, does in fact know her or his benefactor. The Rambam gives an example. He writes of the greatest sages who tied coins into their robes or placed money in the folds of a linen sheet and threw them behind their backs, allowing the poor to approach and to pick the coins from their robes so that the poor would not be ashamed. Thus, if one of the earlier instances of gift-giving would make the person susceptible to embarrassment or shame, this form attempts to preserve the process

---

30. Marion, Jean-Luc, "Sketch of a Phenomenological Concept of Sacrifice," in *The Reason of the Gift*, trans. Stephen E. Lewis (Charlottesville: University of Virginia Press, 2011), 70–72.

of gift-giving while short-circuiting the structure in which shame or embarrassment might emerge. In some sense, there is also some resistance to the allures of pride because the focus is on the other not being ashamed—and not because I could still feel a kind of self-satisfaction in doing something for another.

In short, from the perspective of the giver, the givee is unknown, and in Marion's terms, the gift is accomplished without my intentional relation to the givee, showing that the gift still takes place "without" the concrete or "empirical," "transcendent" givee.[31]

The "next" level in Maimonides's declination of the gift and gift-giving also remains within what Marion would regard as the gift within his peculiar "reduction." In this case, we have the bracketing of the giver, though the gift remains the gift, even if the giver is not present or not known. In this case, someone knows to whom he or she gives, but the givee does not know his or her benefactor. As an example, the Rambam cites the greatest sages who used to walk about in secret and put coins in or at the doors of the poor. Because they are unknown, the incognito giving prevents or at least attenuates any repayment and, in its own way, forestalls a feeling of pride where another would recognize what I do. Again, the gift remains the gift even when the concrete giver is absent.

The penultimate level of gift-giving, but highest within this sphere, also remains within what we might call (for Marion) a double reduction. This occurs when both giver and givee are "bracketed," or when, for Maimonides, one gives without knowing to whom one gives, and without the recipient knowing from whom he received. This has the effect of only leaving in play not the "gift," *but giving for the sake of itself.* In some sense, I do not give for my sake or to be recognized by the other; I do not give to recognize the other in his or her individuality (the real, "empirical" individuals). Rather, I give for the sake of the "mitzvah" itself. (The most literal rendition of mitzvah is "command," but it also has the connotations of and is often rendered colloquially as "good deed," and as such can include any sort of charitable act.)

The point here is that I perform the mitzvah only for the sake of the mitzvah, not for any external consequences. (Maimonides gives a his-

---

31. Marion, *Étant donné*, 136; *Being Given*, 94. "The givee is governed by the givenness of the gift, and the giver plays—phenomenologically and not in terms of [the] natural attitude—the role of a givee: it is to him that the gift is given to appear. Thus even without the givee, the gift is accomplished; for it is enough that it give *itself* for it to show *itself.*"

torical example of the "anonymous fund," or the "Chamber of Secrets," that was set up in the Holy Temple in Jerusalem where the righteous gave in secret and the poor profited in secret. This can likewise take shape when one gives to a charity fund.) Accordingly, we find similar expressions of this in the Jewish tradition. For example, in the *Mishnah, Pirkei Avot*, it is written that the reward of a mitzvah is doing another mitzvah (4:2), and in the Chassidic text, the *Tanya*, it is also written that the reward for a mitzvah is brought about by the mitzvah itself.[32] I am not getting anything out of doing the mitzvah. This certainly challenges an economic interpretation of the gift!

It is important to note that doing a mitzvah for the sake of a mitzvah implies that this is not an arbitrary decision to give on my part. As a command, I am commanded from a *source other than myself*. Evidently, for Maimonides, the command has a religious source, from the Holy. But again, the fulfillment of the command here is not the termination of an obligation, but the gaining of a command to do "another" command, good deed, or charitable act. This binds me to another in an important way, and it is why the sages will link the Hebrew term *mitzvah* to the Aramaic term *tzavta*, which means attaching or connecting or companionship. A mitzvah connects the person who is commanded *to the One who commands*.[33] In its own way, the mitzvah is an interpersonal gift that emerges for and from the interpersonal relation. In doing the mitzvah, I am connected to the One who commands.

The Hebrew expression "mitzvah," by virtue of its very structure and occurrence, is more than a secular command, good deed, or teaching; this is because of the divine participation from which it springs and which it elicits. For this reason, it might be compared in a Christian context to a "sacrament." In Jean-Yves Lacoste's work that touches on givenness, the given, and the gift, sacramentality has its own style of givenness, peculiar to what I call the sphere of "feeling" or the "heart" and what he calls "affection" or "affectivity"; it can be given only in its own terms and is not received in object-presentation or susceptible to measures imposed by us. As received, it is the intertwining of the

---

32. Rabbi Schneur Zalman of Liadi, *Likutei Amarim (Tanya)* (Bilingual Edition) (New York: Kehot Publication Society, 1984), Chapter 37.

33. Torah Ohr (Rabbi Schneur Zalman of Liadi), Genesis 6b: "'and He commanded us,' from the term tzavta and connection with the Infinite Light, source of the mitzvot above."

giving and the given, as divine gift in history, from and for participation, for becoming holy.[34]

The point I want to make with this is that on this level of gift-giving, the motivating factors are not the giver, the givee, or the object, "gift"; it is for the sake of the mitzvah itself *insofar as* it binds me to the source of the mitzvah itself. It constitutes a "religious," vertical moment in gift-giving. So although it may (erroneously) seem that doing a mitzvah can be done outside of loving, the point of the mitzvah, from already loving, is to evoke loving, and because it issues from a command, which is inherently relational and vertical, it is implicitly from "religious" loving that this gift-giving ensues.

Without trying unduly to force a connection between Maimonides and Marion, I do think we can see striking parallels here between this level of gift-giving and the third bracketing in Marion. What is exposed in his "reduction" of the gift is the giveability itself. As Marion writes, giveability does not merely permit the gift to give itself—this would be arbitrary—"it demands it. . . . Paradoxically, it is the demand for givenness exerted by the givable that makes the gift, and not the giver who yields to it (or not)."[35] "Demanding" in this way determines the giver and the gift, which is further revealed in terms of the ability to accept and receive the gift. Thus, the gift is reduced to the demand for givenness. To this extent, I follow Marion's account.

In Maimonides, the command or demand is not abstract or an anonymous demand because implicitly in the mitzvah there is a religious dimension to the command as from One who commands; in this way, the "demand" of giveability has a more personal, and as I would say, a "vertical" resonance. But because the religious is not merely religious, but moral, the moral, then, is not merely a humanistic "ethics," but delimits or opens up to the religious as its source. Again, the point of the (ethical) mitzvah is implicitly on the order of a religious loving because in doing the mitzvah, it connects the doer to the source of the command or good deed.

However—and this undoubtedly strikes the reader of Maimonides as curious—the fullest expression of the gift takes us beyond even this level of gift-giving, and I suggest beyond what both Derrida and Marion have articulated in their descriptions of the gift.

---

34. Jean-Yves Lacoste, *Être en danger* (Paris: Les Éditions du Cerf, 2011), esp. 61, 70, 114–15, 119, 183–88, 302–7, 324–25.

35. Marion, *Étant donné*, 254; *Being Given*, 107–108.

The Greatest Kind of Giving

It might seem for us that the "highest" point of gift-giving is doing a mitzvah for its own sake and thus being connected in the command to the Source of the command, without any regard for the particularity of oneself or another. (If it stopped here, would this, in its own way, not align itself with what we encountered in Heidegger and Henry?) As it is articulated in the gift-giving for Maimonides, the movement of being connected in the command to the Source of the command is undoubtedly a "religious" moment, I would say. Or, in terms of the earlier exposition, it might be seen that there is nothing higher than what we have already undertaken in terms of a deconstruction (Derrida) and a reduction (Marion) of the gift.

But interestingly, Maimonides describes one form of gift-giving that is superior to all of these described thus far, even the last. I suggest, however, that it is superior or the "highest" in the sense that it fulfills the latter in a unique way. This is because the connection with the "Source" is realized here as the connection with the other person. It is the intertwining *"de-limitation"* of the religious (interpersonal) and the moral (interpersonal) spheres of experience. Without this highest form of gift-giving, the "religious" moment of "giveability" would be abstract, or in terms I have used for Heidegger, "esoteric." For now, however, let me follow Maimonides in his description.

The greatest level, writes the Rambam, the greatest level of gift-giving, above which there is no greater, is to enter into a *partnership with* others, supporting them by endowing them with a gift or loan or finding employment for this person to strengthen him until he needs *no longer to be dependent* upon others. It is not about the gift. If we do find an essential structure of giveability and acceptability, as Marion suggests, for Maimonides, this is essentially connected to interpersonal participation and liberation from restrictions (in principle, from restrictions of all kinds, material, egoic, spiritual, etc.). Thus, what is unique to him is that the "religious moment" of giveability and acceptability is realized in interpersonal relations (and what I clarify in another work as within loving's movement).

In other words, what is essential to Maimonides's thought of the gift is not the deconstruction of the economy of exchange—though he could be seen to be critical of this from the standpoint of the highest form; it is not the anonymity of the giver or the benefactor; it is not the bracketing of transcendences; it is not reducing the putative pure gift to givenness. *It is not about the gift.* Rather, it is the *interpersonal relation that is oriented toward the liberation* of other persons. Gift-giving joins with the other while leaving the integrity of the other *as* it realizes the command as being connected to the Source of the command. It is the *intertwining* of the "moral" and "religious" dimensions of experience.

This form of giving is ideal, not in the sense that it cannot be reached, but in the sense that it is the most intimate, essential form of giving (through loving), and such that it can be *realized every day* as the infinite *in the everyday*, and hence is concrete—in terms I used for Henry, it would be *doing-acts*. It is not the epistemic factor (of being known or unknown), but the interpersonal relation that is essential, that is called forth from the other, and that frees the other to become who he or she is/becoming. Gift-giving constitutes *an intervention* (a personal interpersonal intervention) in loving that liberates. Thus, there is a direct concern with the other person, from the other, for the other person—*and not a concern with the gift as such.* There is a direct "relation" with the other person that allows the gift to emerge as gift, for me as lover, and for the other as beloved, in humility.

There are a few implications I want to draw at this stage. First, essential to this movement is the direct *participation with* another and *liberation* as de-limitation or redemption. Although I am not suggesting that Maimonides uses the expressions of loving and beloved that I employ here, Loving, and the interpersonal loving of beloveds, is presupposed in his account of the gift, and this harbors at its core both "participation with" others and "liberation" from material and spiritual restrictions. It expresses the gift from the perspective of loving and the beloved interpersonally. For Maimonides, it is not whether something is a gift or constitutes a gift—again, it is not about the gift—but it concerns the interpersonal nexus in which a gift can become a gift. The meaning of the gift is fully realized as gift, as "pure" gift, not through a worry about economy (because it is eclipsed here) and not with further and further reductions (though it is "reduced" in a new way), but through the direct involvement with another person toward her or his liberation as from the Source of loving. And as interpersonal, it also implies our own liberation from material and spiritual restrictions. This participation and liberation would be structurally different from a distorted sense of sacrifice in which I destroyed a good or others in a putative attempt "to free" them or myself. At the very least, that would be expression of pride. [36]

It would also be an expression of pride to take ourselves too seriously in this "participation"—as if we were the only source, as it were—even though this "moral" vertical dimension is a responsiveness to others. It is intertwined from the very outset with the religious, vertical Source. Our participation with/liberation is already as from another. To put it in terms of Michel Henry that we saw in Chapter 3, it is not merely an *acting*, nor reductively only a *doing*, but "doing-acts" of *tzedakah*. This relates to the second point.

If the highest form of gift-giving here can be said to be constitutive of the moral or interpersonal sphere, then the latter can be said to be the fulfillment of the religious and the religious command/connection. This is not to say this "highest" form is a reduction of the religious to the so-called humanistic ethical. The religious is still functional in what I am calling here the moral sphere: although the moral is not possible without the religious, the religious is abstract without the moral. Put in still different terms, although carrying out the command (mitzvah) connects us to the Source of the command, which itself is evocative of loving, the command is accomplished by loving as freely given. In loving others, we are loving God. Carrying out the command for its own sake, then, is de-limited as loving when we participate with others toward liberation.

---

36. See Steinbock, *Moral Emotions*, Chapters 1 and 7. See Marion, *The Reason of the Gift*, 70–72.

Conclusion

In Chapter 1, I clarified surprise as an emotion and distinguished a surprise from a gift, describing the gift's possibility of emergence through its givenness in humility. Chapter 2 described in Heidegger a sheer emergent giving peculiar to the eventing *Ereignis*, explicating the "*It* gives." The uniqueness of the individual and individuation is lost in sheer giving, resulting in a possible esotericism removed from interpersonal experience and thus from the "moral" sphere of existence. In contrast to Heidegger, I noted that within the Abrahamic tradition, even the mystics, who putatively "retreat" and seek God or the ineffable Godhead, do not recoil into an esotericism (Being without beings); rather, for them, the so-called retreat is immediately and directly *connected to the love of the stranger or the participation with the neighbor.*

Curiously, this line of thought dealing with the problem of machination is played out in an explicitly religious context in Henry's work when our human situation is diagnosed as the problem of an induced, given forgetfulness. Although Henry's thought does occur in a religious context, this "problem" is curiously not portrayed—as one might suspect—in religious or moral terms as "idolatry" or even as "pride," for which we as human persons would be responsible. Here in Henry's work, giving and the "gift of Life" are ultimately reducible to the revelatory self-affecting immanence of absolute Life. It leaves problematic the question concerning the meaning of transcendence or of the world as what is given in a manifest way.

Chapter 4 took up the problem of givenness in terms of Marion's articulation of saturation, whose core meaning is revelation. The problem of givenness was approached from the other side of the experience—not from the religious or the saturated phenomenon—but from the side of the so-called "poor phenomenon." I described four ways in which the poverty of the poor phenomenon could be understood—all of which point to what I understand as vertical de-limiting experiences.

In Chapter 5, I turned to Derrida's and Marion's debate about the gift in order then to resituate the problem of the gift, not only in terms of Maimonides's delineation of gift-giving, but within the deepest sense of gift-giving, which concerns the interpersonal relation. This "highest" form of gift-giving in Maimonides does not premise the meaning of the gift on the anonymity of the giver, the givee, or the giveability of the gift itself. Rather, it is a direct encounter, intervention, and what is more, *participation with* another from loving; it is a personal (unique, absolute) relation in this most radical sense of an inter*personal* relation such that it can never be anonymous. It is a fulfillment of a relation to the source of the mitzvah itself, signifying the intertwining of the religious and moral spheres of experience.

We can agree with Derrida that a subject never purely gives or receives a gift and that the "subject" and "object" are arrested effects of the gift. But for me, this is the case for different reasons. It is not because the pure gift is the figure of the impossible, but because there are no "subjects" who are involved in gift-giving in the first place; further, the very dynamic described by Derrida ignores the relation between mitzvah/loving and humility in which the gift can appear and be received in an interpersonal and inter-Personal nexus.

The "intending" a gift or "meaning" to give a gift is problematic, but again not for the reasons Derrida names. The very experiential reality of the gift (for the gift to be a gift) is such that I do not intend the gift; instead, I "intend" the other person. *But this formulation must be immediately qualified.* Because the person is not an object and loving is a movement in the mode of vertical revelation, not presentation, strictly speaking I do not intend the person ("intend" in the sense of an objectifying act; "person" in the sense of an objective sense). But this is not because we can bracket the giver, the givee, or the gift and in this way short-circuit an economy of giving.

If we are content to use the expression "intentionality" to cover the variegated field of givenness and evidence—as I have suggested in other works—then we would have to say (along with Levinas) that the subject-object relation is not the only kind of intentionality. Marion, of course, would agree because he himself has described various kinds of saturated intentionality. The point, however, is that if the gift appears (or cannot appear) as such, it is not because I intend *it*, but because the gift occurs in direct loving participation with another, and where the recipient is concerned, in humility. I even receive Myself, as not self-grounding, in humility.[1] The issue is not whether the gift can (or cannot) be relieved from an economy, because what is uneconomic in this dynamic is *loving*. Even a "loving response" is itself creatively, freely initiated on the ground of loving—generative—not an exchange and not a reaction like an effect to a cause.

Accordingly, the beloved is *revealed* in loving in which the gift *manifests* itself. For Derrida, I am occupied *with the gift*, and as a consequence there is the problem of an economic counter-gift. It is then submitted that the gift could be a gift as such only if it were to arise spontaneously without past or remembering, without future or anticipation, without awareness "of" it, without interaction, without attendees—rejoining in its own way Heidegger's sheer eventing, sheer taking place taking place.

It has been argued that it is the gift that creates a "feeling-bond" or emotional tie; it is the gift that has the power to bind people together.[2] It is no doubt true that I might become closer to another through a gift, but at root I cannot give a gift to become closer to another without the gift eclipsing itself and without mitigating the very relation I am trying to establish. More importantly, I have sought to show that it is only through the interpersonal relation or "bond" *already accomplished through*, for example, loving and humility—but also through other "moral emotions" such as sympathy, trust, repentance, and so on—that the gift can arise in the first place.[3]

This is not to say that one loves and so on to help someone with a "gift." As Max Scheler points out in a different context, loving is not based in its "usefulness." Rather, one loves the other person as bearer of value, and the gift (from sacrifice to mitzvah or sacrament), if it helps, is simply an expression of that loving. The "gift" is grounded in interpersonal loving, which has its deepest source in infinite inter-Personal Loving or holiness. One loves out of ebullient fullness being drawn from ever-higher value-bearers, not from self-renunciation—

---

1. See Steinbock, *Moral Emotions*, Chapter 7.
2. See for example, Hyde, *The Gift*, 72, 89–90, 92.
3. See Steinbock, *Moral Emotions*; see this work, Chapter 1.

which would be a symptom of ressentiment, self-escape, and possibly self-hate.[4]

For me, the gift is not the point of the gift. The "point" is the relation of lover to beloved, which allows the gift to appear, and dare I say, "as such." It is true that the "gift" appears only when it is not focal, but this is because I am already *occupied by another*, most profoundly, in a personal manner.[5] This does not mean that the gift is the figure of the impossible—it would become "impossible" or distracted from itself, as it were, only if I were to intend the gift for its sake and not instead being *devoted to* another *from the other, toward their generative flourishing*. It is here that the "gift" becomes most deeply the "matter" in Heidegger's and Shakespeare's sense as the "between whom" that emerges in and through the interpersonal relation.

Although bracketing the direct person-to-person relation in various forms can still be counted among the kinds of gift-giving for Maimonides, the deepest sense of the gift-giving is not attained by such bracketing of the giver, the givee, or even the gift. In fact, the danger is that removing such "transcendencies" might just result in suspending all involvement with others! To stay with the language of the gift, it is not that "you" are bracketed in the reduction to givability, but that "you"— uniquely—are already the beloved for whom I would *give up* my-self, which is realizing Myself as interpersonal, in which the gift can appear as such.

As opposed to what Scheler would term a ressentiment "offering," a "positive" sacrifice emerges from inner spiritual or bodily depth and vitality such that the deeper and more central the sacrifice, the more indifferent persons are to their "fate" in the peripheral areas of their existence and the more indifferent they are to the gift because it serves the others in a de-limiting way. They do not intervene in a struggle because of negative values of, say, poverty, sickness, unhappiness, ugliness (which would be signs of ressentiment), but they join with or accompany another in, say, poverty to develop whatever may be positive, and thus "despite" the things that are bearers of negative values. They do not love such a life, Scheler continues, because it is sick, poor, unhappy, or repugnant, but love what is "behind" them, as it were, through a deeper feeling of life, vigor, and beauty. Helping and benevo-

---

4. Max Scheler, *Ressentiment*, trans. Lewis B. Coser and William W. Holdheim (Milwaukee, WI: Marquette University Press, 2007), 58–60.

5. See Steinbock, *Phenomenology and Mysticism*, regarding experience in St. Teresa of Avila.

lence are the consequences of loving participation, with the hope that the other persons can possibly be relieved of bearers of negative values by moving toward and being guided by bearers of higher spiritual and vital values.[6] What we are dealing with, then, is the "whole" in which loving unfolds and of which the gift becomes an expression. If the *mitzvah* (the command or the good deed) binds me to the *source* of mitzvah itself, then participation with the neighbor or stranger is another angle on this binding. This direct *participation* with the other for Maimonides implies further what might be called the *Exodus event*. I participate with the other "so that" together we can "leave Egypt," that is, in our orientation to higher or deeper absolute, "personal" values, we are "then" freed from material and spiritual restrictions, as is conveyed in the single Hebrew term—מצרים—*mitzraim/metzarim*—Egypt/limitations.[7]

But again, this loving is not "useful" or pragmatic; it issues from overabundant Loving. If our loving is turned toward those "in need" or "suffering," it is not bent on the need or the suffering, but from and toward those others as bearers of value. The gift echoes or is the expression of the liberating de-limiting movement of loving. The exemplarity of the movement of loving and its revealing of higher values can help to point the way from more restricting values that serve to enslave, and in the reorientation, to let all levels of experienced value be fulfilling in their own way. To participate, accompany, or comfort others in one respect, then, in and of itself can free others to be more open to more encompassing dimensions in other respects. This points in its own way to reception in humility, to the experience of being not self-grounding in the interpersonal and inter-Personal spheres, and to the *ways* in which we receive ourselves vocationally.

The giving is not for the sake of the gift or for the sake of givenness. Giving serves the connection; it does not establish it: the gift emerges from the connection without being the object of it. The point therefore is not to liberate *the gift* from terms of the exchange as Marion suggests.[8] But it does mean that participation expressed in gift-giving is oriented toward the other and thereby elicits co-liberation, releasing, or

---

6. Scheler, *Ressentiment*, 60–61.
7. See Steinbock, *Phenomenology and Mysticism*, esp. Chapters 2 and 8.
8. Marion, *Étant donné*, 122: "Si l'*epochē* parvient à traiter le don, elle s'exercera en le libérant des termes de l'échange et du statut d'objet, tous transcendants." *Being Given*, 84.

redemption, which is to say, the interpersonal/inter-Personal nexus. In contemporary liberation theology, philosophy of liberation, and liberation psychology, it can be understood as the process of *acompañamiento*, or accompanying others. Accompaniment is the reorientation of interpersonal relations, a practice of being with others to listen, to witness, to advocate in the effort of liberation in its myriad forms and implications.[9]

These critical reflections on the gift have served as a leading clue to the phenomenon of loving, even though it is from loving that the gift acquires its very significance as gift. In subsequent works, I describe loving as vertical movement, as de-limiting, such that it connects all the vertical modes of givenness in their difference and founds hating and its modalities. It also opens to the dimension of revelatory experience that concerns vocations and exemplars.

---

9.   See the incisive presentation of and contribution to this movement by Mary Watkins, "Psychosocial Accompaniment," *Journal of Social and Political Psychology* 3, no. 1 (2015): 324–41. See Steinbock, "The Role of the Moral Emotions in Our Social and Political Practices," in Special Issue: *Phenomenology and the Post-Secular Turn: Reconsidering the "Return of the Religious,"* ed. Michael Staudigl and Rowland Stout, *International Journal of Philosophical Studies* 24 (2016): 600–614.

Bibliography

Alvis, Jason W. *Marion and Derrida on The Gift and Desire: Debating the Generosity of Things*. Dordrecht: Springer, 2016.

Aristotle. *Metaphysics*, Books I–IV. Translated by Hugh Tredennick. Cambridge, MA: Harvard University Press, 1933.

———. *Poetics*. Edited and translated by Stephen Halliwell. Cambridge, MA: Harvard University Press, 1995.

Assheuer, Thomas. *Die Zeit*, N° 12/2014. March 21, 2014.

Augustine, *De Trinitate*.

Bernet, Rudolf. "Christianity and Philosophy." In *The Philosophy of Michel Henry*. Edited by Anthony J. Steinbock. *Continental Philosophy Review* 32, no. 3 (1999): 325–42.

Buber, Martin. "Ich und Du." In *Das dialogische Prinzip*. Heidelberg: Lambert Schneider, 1965.

Caputo, John D. and Michael J. Scanlon, eds. *God, the Gift, and Postmodernism*. Bloomington, IN: Indiana University Press, 1999.

Coles, Romand. *Rethinking Generosity: Critical Theory and the Politics of Caritas*. Ithaca, NY: Cornell University Press, 1997.

Dastur, Françoise. "Time, Event, and Presence in the Late Heidegger." *Continental Philosophy Review* 47, no. 3–4 (2014): 399–421.

Davidson, Donald. *Problems of Rationality*. Oxford: Oxford University Press, 2004.

———. "Rational Animals." *Dialectica* 36 (1982): 318–27.

Dennett, Daniel. "Surprise, Surprise," Commentary on O'Regan and Noe. *Behavioral and Brain Sciences* 24, no. 5 (2001): 982.

Depraz, Natalie. "Seeking a Phenomenological Metaphysics: Henry's Reference to Meister Eckhart." Translated by Gregory B. Sadler. In *The Philosophy of Michel Henry*. Edited by Anthony J. Steinbock. *Continental Philosophy Review* 32, no. 3 (1999): 303–24.

———. "Surprise, Valence, Emotion: The Multivectorial Integrative Cardio-Phenomenology of Surprise." In *Surprise: An Emotion*, edited by Natalie Depraz and Anthony J. Steinbock. Dordrecht: Springer Publishers, forthcoming.

Derrida, Jacques. *Donner le temps. 1. La fausse monnaie*. Paris: Galilée, 1991.

131

————. *Given Time: 1. Counterfeit Money*. Translated by Peggy Kamuf. Chicago: University of Chicago Press, 1992.

————. *L'écriture et la différence*. Paris: Seuil, 1967.

————. *Writing and Difference*. Translated by Alan Bass. Chicago: University of Chicago Press, 1978.

Derrida, Jacques and Jean-Luc Marion. "On the Gift." In *God, the Gift, and Postmodernism*. Edited by John D. Caputo and Michael J. Scanlon, 54–78. Bloomington, IN: Indiana University Press, 1999.

Descartes, René. *The Passions of the Soul*. Translated by Stephen Voss. Indianapolis, IN: Hackett Publishing Company, 1989.

Dobh Baer of Lubavitch. *Tract on Ecstasy*. Translated by Louis Jacobs. London: Vallentine Mitchell, 1963.

Farías, Victor. *Heidegger and Nazism*. Translated by Paul Burrell and Gabriel R. Ricci. Philadelphia: Temple University Press, 1989.

————. *Heidegger et le nazisme*. Translated from Spanish and German by Myriam Benarroch and Jean-Baptiste Grasset. Paris: Verdier, 1987.

Frankl, Viktor E. *Man's Search for Meaning*. Translated by Ilse Lasch. Boston: Beacon Press, 2006.

Gschwandtner, Christina M. *Degrees of Givenness: On Saturation in Jean-Luc Marion*. Bloomington, IN: Indiana University Press, 2014.

Gutierrez, Gustavo. *A Theology of Liberation: History, Politics, and Salvation*. New York: Orbis Books, 1973.

Hanson, Jeffrey and Michael R. Kelly. "The Idea of Phenomenology: Immanence, Givenness and Reflection." In *Michel Henry: The Affects of Thought*. Edited by Jeffrey Hanson and Michael R. Kelly. New York: Bloomsbury, 2014.

Hart, James. "A Phenomenological Theory and Critique of Culture: A Reading of Michel Henry's *La barbarie*." In *The Philosophy of Michel Henry*. Edited by Anthony J. Steinbock. *Continental Philosophy Review* 32, no. 3 (1999): 255–70.

Hart, Kevin. "Torah, God and Idol." In *Ancient Israelite Philosophy*. Edited by Alex Kohav (forthcoming).

Heidegger, Martin. *Anmerkungen I–V (Schwarze Hefte 1942–1948)*, Gesamtausgabe 97. Edited by Peter Trawny. Frankfurt am Main: Vittorio Klostermann, 2015.

————. *Beiträge zur Philosophie (Vom Ereignis)*, Gesamtausgabe 65. Edited by Friedrich-Wilhelm von Herrmann. Frankfurt: Vittorio Klostermann, 1989.

————. *Die Grundbegriffe der Metaphysik. Welt-Endlichkeit-Einsamkeit*, Gesamtausgabe 29/30. Edited by Friedrich-Wilhelm von Herrmann. Frankfurt am Main, 1983.

————. *Feldweg-Gespräche (1944/45)*, Gesamtausgabe 77. Edited by Ingrid Schüssler, 2nd ed. Frankfurt am Main: Vittorio Klostermann, 2007.

————. *Holzwege*. 6th ed. Frankfurt am Main: Klostermann, 1980.

————. *Identität und Differenz (1955–1957)*, Gesamtausgabe 11. Edited by Friedrich-Wilhelm v. Herrmann. Frankfurt am Main: Vittorio Klostermann, 2006.

————. *Time and Being*. Translated by Joan Stambaugh. New York: Harper and Row, 1977.

————. *Überlegungen II–VI (Schwarze Hefte 1931–1938)*, Gesamtausgabe 94. Edited by Peter Trawny. Frankfurt am Main: Vittorio Klostermann, 2014.

————. *Überlegungen VI–XI (Schwarze Hefte 1938/39)*, Gesamtausgabe 95. Edited by Peter Trawny. Frankfurt am Main: Vittorio Klostermann, 2014.

————. *Überlegungen XII–XV (Schwarze Hefte 1939–1941)*, Gesamtausgabe 96. Edited by Peter Trawny. Frankfurt am Main: Vittorio Klostermann, 2014.

————. *Zur Sache des Denkens (1962–1964)*. Gesamtausgabe 14. Edited by Friedrich-Wilhelm v. Herrmann. Frankfurt am Main: Kostermann, 2007.

Heinämaa, Sara. "Love and Admiration (Wonder): Fundaments of the Self-Other Relations." In *Emotional Experiences: Ethical and Social Significance*, edited by John J.

Drummond and Sonja Rinofner-Kreidl, 155–74. London: Rowman & Littlefield, 2018.

Held, Klaus. "Fundamental Moods and Heidegger's Critique of Contemporary Culture." Translated by Anthony J. Steinbock. In *Reading Heidegger: Commemorations*. Edited by John Sallis. Bloomington: Indiana University Press, 1993.

Henry, Michel. *C'est moi la vérité: pour une philosophie du christianisme*. Paris: Seuil, 1996.

———. *The Essence of Manifestation*. Translated by Girard Etzkorn. The Hague: Martinus Nijhoff, 1973.

———. *I Am the Truth: Toward a Philosophy of Christianity*. Translated by Susan Emanuel. Stanford University Press, 2002.

———. *Incarnation: A Philosophy of Flesh*. Translated by Karl Hefty. Evanston, IL: Northwestern University Press, 2015.

———. *Incarnation: une philosophie de la chair*. Paris: Seuil, 2000.

———. *La barbarie*. Paris: Grasset, 1987.

———. *L'essence de la manifestation*. 2nd ed. Paris: PUF, 1990.

———. *Marx*. Paris: Gallimard, 1976.

Horner, Robyn. *Rethinking God as Gift: Marion, Derrida, and the Limits of Phenomenology*. New York: Fordham University Press, 2001.

Husserl, Edmund. *Analyses Concerning Passive and Active Synthesis: Lectures on Transcendental Logic*. Translated by Anthony J. Steinbock. Dordrecht: Kluwer, 2001.

Hyde, Lewis. *The Gift: Creativity and the Artist in the Modern World*. New York: Vintage Books, 2007.

Jaspers, Karl. *Die Schuldfrange: Ein Beitrage zur deutschen Frage*. Munich: Piper Verlag, 1947/1965.

———. *The Question of German Guilt*. Translated by E. B. Ashton. New York: Fordham University Press, 2000.

Kant, Immanuel. *Anthropologie in pragmatischer Hinsicht*. Edited by Karl Vorländer. Hamburg: Felix Meiner, 1980.

———. *Kritik der Urteilskraft*. Edited by Karl Vorländer. Hamburg: Felix Meiner, 1974.

Lacoste, Jean-Yves. *Être en danger*. Paris: Les Éditions du Cerf, 2011.

Laoureux, Sébastien. *L'immanence à la limite: recherches sur la phénoménologie de Michel Henry*. Paris: Les Éditions du Cerf, 2005.

Lévinas, Emmanuel. "Being Jewish." Translated by Mary Beth Mader. *Continental Philosophy Review* 40, 2007.

Luther, Arthur R. "Original Emergence in Heidegger and Nishida." *Philosophy Today*, 26, no. 4/4 (1982): 345–56.

Maimonides, *The Code of Maimonides, Book Seven: The Book of Agriculture*. Translated by Isaac Klein. New Haven, CT: Yale University Press, 1979.

Maraldo, John. "Nothing Gives: Marion and Nishida on Gift-giving and God." In *Japanese and Continental Philosophy: Conversations with the Kyoto School*. Edited by Bret W. Davis, Brian Schroeder, and Jason M. Wirth. Bloomington, IN: Indiana University Press, 2011.

Marion, Jean-Luc. *Dieu sans l'être*. Paris: PUF, 1991.

———. *Being Given: Toward a Phenomenology of Givenness*. Translated by Jeffrey L. Kosky. Stanford, CA: Stanford University Press, 2002.

———. *De surcroît: études sur les phénomènes saturés*. Paris: PUF, 2001.

———. *Étant donné: essai d'une phenomenologie de la donation*. Paris: PUF, 1997.

———. *God without Being*. Translated by David Tracy. Chicago: Chicago University Press, 1991.

————. *In Excess: Studies of Saturated Phenomena.* Translated by Robyn Horner and Vincent Berraud. New York: Fordham University Press, 2002.

————. *The Reason of the Gift.* Translated by Stephen E. Lewis. Charlottesville: University of Virginia Press, 2011.

————. *Reduction and Givenness: Investigations of Husserl, Heidegger, and Phenomenology.* Translated by Thomas A. Carlson. Evanston, IL: Northwestern University Press, 1998.

————. *Réduction et donation: recherches sur Husserl, Heidegger et la phénoménologie.* Paris: PUF, 1989.

————. "Sketch of a Phenomenological Concept of Sacrifice." In *The Reason of the Gift.* Translated by Stephen E. Lewis. Charlottesville: University of Virginia Press, 2011.

Mauss, Marcel. "Essai sur le don. Forme et raison de l'échange dans les societies archaïques." *Sociologie et anthropologie.* Paris: PUF, 1989/1950.

————. *The Gift: The Form and Reason for Exchange in Archaic Societies.* Translated by W. D. Halls. New York: W. W. Norton & Company, 2000.

Sartre, Jean-Paul. *Cahiers pour une morale.* Paris: Gallimard, 1983.

————. *L'Être et le néant: Essai d'ontologie phénoménologique.* Paris: Gallimard, 1943.

Scheler, Max. *Die Formalismus in der Ethik und die materiale Wertethik.* Edited by Maria Scheler. München: Francke Verlag, 1966.

————. *Die Idee des Friedens und der Pazifismus.* Berlin: Der Neue Geist, 1931.

————. *Ressentiment.* Translated by Lewis B. Coser and William W. Holdheim. Milwaukee, WI: Marquette University Press, 2007.

————. *Vom Ewigen im Menschen*, Gesammelte Werke, vol. 5. Edited by Maria Scheler. Bern: Francke Verlag, 1954.

————. *Vom Umsturz der Werte: Abhandlungen und Aufsätze.* Edited by Maria Scheler. Bern: Francke Verlag, 1955.

Schirmacher, Wolfgang. *Technik und Gelassenheit: Zeitkritik nach Heidegger.* Munich: Alber, 1983.

Shakespeare. *Hamlet.* In *The Complete Works of William Shakespeare.* Edited by David Bevington. Glenview, IL: Scott, Foresman and Company, 1980.

Smith, Adam. *The Early Writings of Adam Smith.* Edited by J. Ralph Lindgren. New York: Augustus M. Kelly, 1967.

Steinbock, Anthony J. *Home and Beyond: Generative Phenomenology after Husserl.* Evanston, IL: Northwestern University Press, 1995.

————. "Interpersonal Attention through Exemplarity," *Journal of Consciousness Studies: Beyond Ourselves.* Edited by Evan Thompson (2001), 179–96.

————. *Limit-Phenomena and Phenomenology in Husserl.* London: Rowman & Littlefield, 2017.

————. *Moral Emotions: Reclaiming the Evidence of the Heart.* Evanston, Il: Northwestern University Press, 2014.

————. *Phenomenology and Mysticism: The Verticality of Religious Experience.* Bloomington, IN: Indiana University Press, 2007.

————. "The Role of the Moral Emotions in Our Social and Political Practices." Special Issue: *Phenomenology and the Post-Secular Turn: Reconsidering the 'Return of the Religious.'* Edited by Michael Staudigl and Rowland Stout. *International Journal of Philosophical Studies* 24 (2016): 600–614.

————. "Saturated Intentionality." In *The Body: Classic and Contemporary Readings.* Edited by Donn Welton. London: Blackwell, 1999.

Teresa of Avila, Saint. *The Collected Works of St. Teresa of Avila*, Vol. 1. Translated by Kieran Kavanaugh, O.C.D., and Otilio Rodriguez, O.C.D. Washington, DC: ICS Publications, 1976.

————. *The Collected Works of St. Teresa of Avila*, Vol. 2. Translated by Kieran Kavanaugh, O.C.D., and Otilio Rodriguez, O.C.D. Washington, DC: ICS Publications, 1980.

————. *The Collected Works of St. Teresa of Avila*, Vol. 3. Translated by Kieran Kavanaugh, O.C.D., and Otilio Rodriguez, O.C.D. Washington, DC: ICS Publications, 1985.

————. [Teresa de Jesús]. *Obras Completas*. Edited by Efren de La Madre de Dios, O.C.D., and Otger Steggink, O.Carm. Madrid: Biblioteca de Autores Cristianos, 1997.

Trawny, Peter. *Heidegger et l'antisémitisme: Sur les cahiers noirs*. Translated by Julia Christ and Jean-Claude Monod. Paris: Seuil, 2014.

————. *Heidegger und der Mythos der jüdischen Weltverschwörung*. 3rd ed. Frankfurt am Main: Klostermann, 2015.

Watkins, Mary. "Psychosocial Accompaniment." *Journal of Social and Political Psychology* 3, no. 1 (2015): 324–41.

Welten, Ruud. "Jean-Paul Sartre, Notebooks for an Ethics: The Ontology of the Gift." *Journal for Cultural and Religious Theory* 15, no. 1 (Fall 2015): 3–15.

Zahavi, Dan. "Michel Henry and the Phenomenology of the Invisible." *Continental Philosophy Review* 32, no. 3 (1999): 223–40.

Zalman, Rabbi Schneur, of Liadi. *Likutei Amarim (Tanya)*. Bilingual edition. New York: Kehot Publication Society, 1984.

Index

About the Author

Anthony J. Steinbock is Professor of Philosophy and Director of the Phenomenology Research Center at Southern Illinois University, Carbondale. He works in the areas of phenomenology, social ontology, aesthetics, and religious philosophy. His many publications include *Limit-Phenomena and Phenomenology in Husserl* (2017), *Moral Emotions: Reclaiming the Evidence of the Heart* (2014; 2015 Symposium Book Award), *Phenomenology and Mysticism: The Verticality of Religious Experience* (2007/2009; 2009 Edward Goodwin Ballard Book Prize in Phenomenology), and *Home and Beyond: Generative Phenomenology after Husserl* (1995). He is the translator of *Edmund Husserl, Analyses Concerning Passive and Active Synthesis: Lectures on Transcendental Logic* (2001). He serves as Editor-in-Chief, Continental Philosophy Review, and is the General Editor of Northwestern University Press, "SPEP" Series.

www.ingramcontent.com/pod-product-compliance
Lightning Source LLC
Chambersburg PA
CBHW030653270326
41929CB00007B/343